S'

MW01068479

American
ENGLISH FILE

Workbook

Christina Latham-Koenig

Clive Oxenden

Mike Boyle

Paul Seligson and Clive Oxenden are the original co-authors of
English File 1 and *English File 2*

OXFORD
UNIVERSITY PRESS

Contents

Powerful listening and interactive assessment CD-ROM

Your iChecker disc on the inside back cover of this Workbook includes:

- **AUDIO** – Download ALL of the audio files for the Listening and Pronunciation activities in this Workbook for on-the-go listening practice.

- **FILE TESTS** – Check your progress by taking a self-assessment test after you complete each File.

Audio: When you see this symbol iChecker, go to the iChecker disc in the back of this Workbook. Load the disc in your computer.

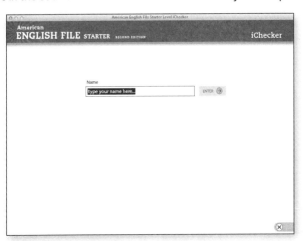

Type your name and press "ENTER."

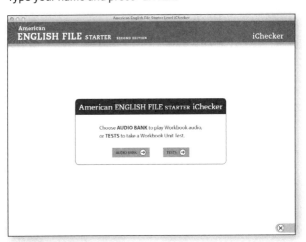

Choose "AUDIO BANK."

3

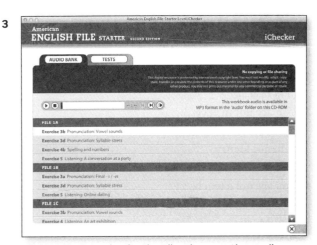

Click on the exercise for the File. Then use the media player to listen.

You can transfer the audio to a mobile device from the "audio" folder on the disc.

File test: At the end of every File, there is a test. To do the test, load the iChecker and select "Tests." Select the test for the File you have just finished.

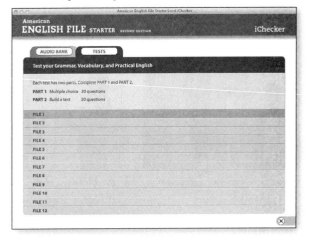

1A Hello!

1 GRAMMAR verb *be*: *I* and *you*

a Rewrite the sentences with contractions.

1 I am Lisa.
  I'm Lisa.

2 You are not in class 3.
  You aren't in class 3.

3 I am not Henry.
  _____

4 You are not a teacher.
  _____

5 I am Maria.
  _____

6 You are in my class.
  _____

7 I am in room 4.
  _____

8 You are not Carlos.
  _____

b Write negative ⊟ sentences or questions ⸮.

1 I'm in class 2. ⊟
  I'm not in class 2.

2 You're a student. ⸮
  Are you a student?

3 I'm Sam. ⊟
  _____

4 You're in my class. ⊟
  _____

5 I'm in room 4. ⸮
  _____

6 You're Liz. ⸮
  _____

7 I'm a teacher. ⊟
  _____

8 You're in class 4. ⸮
  _____

c Complete the dialogues.

1 A Excuse me. *Are you* Andy?
  B No, *I'm not* . I'm Tony.

2 A Hello, *I'm* Jessica.
  B Hi, *I'm* Steve. Nice to meet you.

3 A Hi, _____ Linda. Are you Henry?
  B No, _____ . I'm Max.

4 A Excuse me. _____ in number 8?
  B Yes, _____ . I'm Anna Jones.

5 A Hello. _____ Lisa Gomez?
  B Yes, _____ . Nice to meet you.

6 A Hi. _____ Ben.
  B Hi. _____ Rob.

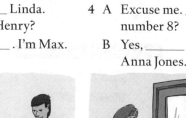

7 A Excuse me. _____ I in room 7?
  B No, _____ . You're in room 8.

8 A Excuse me. _____ my teacher?
  B Yes, _____ . I'm Pete Wilson.

VOCABULARY numbers 0–10; days of the week

Order the letters to make numbers.

1	RUFO	f _ou_ r
2	NET	t _e_ n
3	INNE	n_____e
4	EON	o_____e
5	TEREH	t_____e
6	OWT	t_____o
7	GITHE	e_____t
8	XIS	s_____x
9	ENVSE	s_____n
10	OZRE	z_____o
11	VIEF	f_____e

Write the next word.

1	Friday	Saturday	Sunday	_Monday_
2	Sunday	Monday	Tuesday	_____
3	Tuesday	Monday	Sunday	_____
4	Tuesday	Wednesday	Thursday	_____
5	Friday	Thursday	Wednesday	_____
6	Monday	Tuesday	Wednesday	_____
7	Thursday	Wednesday	Tuesday	_____

PRONUNCIATION word stress; /h/, /aɪ/, and /i/

Underline the stressed syllable.

ex|cuse   he|llo   num|ber   pho|to   re|peat   se|ven

iChecker Listen and check. Then listen again and repeat the words.

Write the words in the chart.

Henry   nice   me   right   meet   hello

h house	aɪ bike	i tree
Henry	_____	_____
_____	_____	_____

iChecker Listen and check. Then listen again and repeat the words.

4 LISTENING

iChecker Listen. Check (✓) the sentence you hear.

1 ____ a Hello, I'm Tony.
  ____ b Hi, I'm Tom.
2 ____ a You're in my class.
  ____ b You aren't in my class.
3 ____ a I'm not a student.
  ____ b I'm a student.
4 ____ a Are you in number 5?
  ____ b Are you in number 9?
5 ____ a Excuse me, what's your name?
  ____ b Sorry, what's your name?
6 ____ a You aren't in class 10.
  ____ b You're in class 2.

USEFUL WORDS AND PHRASES

Learn these words and phrases.

he<u>llo</u>   /hɛˈloʊ/
hi   /haɪ/
I'm   /aɪm/
Nice to meet you.   /naɪs tu mit yu/
What's your name?   /wʌts yɔr neɪm/
Ex<u>cuse</u> me?   /ɪkˈskyuz mi/
<u>Sorry</u>.   /ˈsɑri/
See you soon.   /si yu sun/
good<u>bye</u>   /ɡʊdˈbaɪ/

Ask not what your country can do for you – a
what you can do for your count
John F. Kennedy, US Preside

1 VOCABULARY countries

a Complete the crossword.

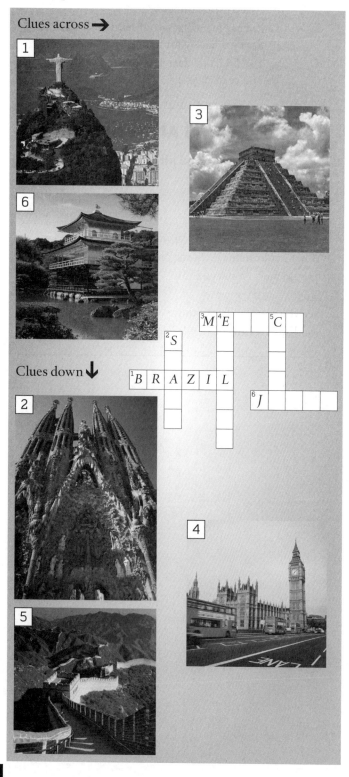

Clues across ➡

Clues down ⬇

³M ⁴E   ⁵C
²S
¹B R A Z I L
⁶J

b Complete the sentences with a country.

1 She's from London. She's from **En**_gland_ .
2 He's from Lima. He's from **P**_____ .
3 I'm from Lisbon. I'm from **P**_____ .
4 You're from Miami. You're from **th**_____
Un_____ **St**_____ .
5 She's from Toronto. She's from **C**_____ .
6 He's from Hanoi. He's from **V**_____ .
7 I'm from Seoul. I'm from **So**_____ **K**_____
8 You're from Santiago. You're from **C**_____ .

2 GRAMMAR verb *be*: *he, she, it*

a Complete the sentences.

1 _She's_ from the United States.

2 _It's_ from China.

3 _____ from Saudi Arabia.

4 _____ from Japan.

5 _____ from Mexico.

6 _____ from Canada.

7 _____ from Spain.

8 _____ from Korea.

b Complete the dialogues with *'s*, *is*, or *isn't*.

1 A ___Is___ Paulo from Portugal?
   B No, he ___isn't___. He _____ from Mexico.
2 A Where _____ Oaxaca? _____ it in Mexico?
   B Yes, it _____.
3 A _____ Yasmin in the Monday class?
   B No, she _____. She _____ in the Tuesday class.
4 A _____ your name Annie?
   B No, it _____. It _____ Anna.

c Write the questions. Then answer with the information in parentheses.

1 Justin Bieber / from Canada? (✔ Ontario)

   Is Justin Bieber from Canada _____ ?

   Yes, he is. He's from Ontario _____ .

2 Hanoi / in China? (✗ Vietnam)

   Is Hanoi in China _____ ?

   No, it isn't. It's in Vietnam _____ .

3 Salma Hayek / from Mexico? (✔ Veracruz)

   _____ ?

   _____ .

4 Lisbon / in Spain? (✗ Portugal)

   _____ ?

   _____ .

5 Copacabana beach / in Brazil? (✔ Rio)

   _____ ?

   _____ .

6 Toronto / in the United States? (✗ Canada)

   _____ ?

   _____ .

7 Cristiano Ronaldo / from Portugal? (✔ Madeira)

   _____ ?

   _____ .

8 Lima / in Mexico? (✗ Peru)

   _____ ?

   _____ .

3 PRONUNCIATION /ɪ/, /oʊ/, and /ɛ/

a Circle the word with a different sound.

fish	1	Brazil	(China)	**E**ngland
phone	2	hell**o**	phot**o**	tw**o**
egg	3	sh**e**	t**e**n	W**e**dnesday

b 🔊 **iChecker** Listen and check. Then listen again and repeat the words.

4 LISTENING

a 🔊 **iChecker** Listen and circle the correct response.

1 a Yes, I am.   (b) I'm from Mexico.
2 a It's in Brazil.   b   No, it isn't.
3 a He's from Peru.   b   She's from Peru.
4 a Yes, I am.   b   No, he isn't.
5 a Yes, it's great.   b   Yes, it's in the US.
6 a No, it's in China.   b   No, I'm not.
7 a He's from London.   b   No, he's from London.
8 a It's in Spain.   b   Yes, he is.

b 🔊 **iChecker** Listen and check your answers.

USEFUL WORDS AND PHRASES

Learn these words and phrases.

Where are you from? /wɛr ɑr yu frʌm/
Where in the US? /wɛr ɪn ðə yuˈɛs/
Let's go! /lɛts goʊ/
<u>mu</u>sic /ˈmyuzɪk/
<u>con</u>cert /ˈkɑnsərt/
to<u>mor</u>row /təˈmɑroʊ/
<u>fa</u>mous /ˈfeɪməs/
<u>sing</u>er /ˈsɪŋər/

Practical English   How do you spell it?

1 THE ALPHABET

a Circle the letter with a different sound.

1 D	E	(I)	V
2 (E)	L	N	X
3 A	G	J	K
4 B	H	P	Z
5 C	F	L	S
6 A	H	J	Y
7 O	Q	U	W
8 F	T	M	S

b **iChecker** Listen and check. Then listen and repeat the letters.

2 VOCABULARY classroom language

a Label the pictures.

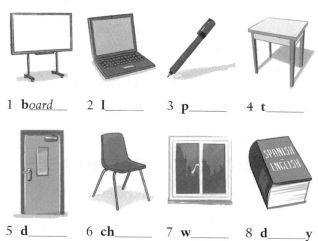

1 b_oard_   2 l_____   3 p_____   4 t_____

5 d_____   6 ch_____   7 w_____   8 d_____y

b Complete the classroom expressions.

go	look	open	~~repeat~~	spell	understand

1 Can you ___repeat___ that, please?
2 _____ at the board, please.
3 _____ your books.
4 Sorry. I don't _____ .
5 How do you _____ it?
6 _____ to page 9.

c Look at the expressions in **b**. Circle the things students say.

3 SPELLING YOUR NAME

a Complete the dialogue with the words from the list.

good	name	last	you	room	Thank
reservation		afternoon		Excuse me?	spell

A ¹ _Good_ afternoon.
B Good ² _____ . I have a ³ _____ .
A What's your ⁴ _____ , please?
B Beth Snowe.
A ⁵ _____
B Beth Snowe.
A How do you ⁶ _____ your ⁷ _____ name?
B S-N-O-W-E.
A ⁸ _____ you. You're in ⁹ _____ 15.
B Thank ¹⁰ _____ .

b Write the words to make questions.

1 How / spell / last name   _How do you spell your_
    last name ?
2 How / spell / first name   _____
3 How / spell / city   _____
4 How / spell / your country   _____

c Answer the questions in **b**. Spell the answers.

1 _____
2 _____
3 _____
4 _____

American women expect to find in their husbands a perfection that English women only hope to find in their butlers.

W. Somerset Maugham, English dramatist & novelist

2A We're Canadian

VOCABULARY nationalities

Complete the puzzle. What's the mystery word?

1 Maria's from Spain. She's **S**panis**h**.

2 Kentaro's from Japan. He's **J**____**e**.

3 Emma's from the UK. She's **B**____**h**.

4 Bianca's from Brazil. She's **Br**____**n**.

5 Jae-won's from Korea. He's **S**____**h K**____**n**.

6 Meiling's from China. She's **C**____**e**.

7 Jorge's from Peru. He's **P**____**n**.

8 William's from England. He's **E**____**h**.

9 Daniela's from Mexico. She's **M**____**n**.

10 Bao's from Vietnam. He's **V**____**e**.

11 Sarah's from Canada. She's **C**____**n**.

12 Mike's from the United States. He's **Am**____**n**.

13 Faisal's from Saudi Arabia. He's **S**____**i**.

GRAMMAR verb be: we, you, they

Write affirmative ⊞ sentences. Use contractions.

1 we / from Spain
  We're from Spain .

2 you / in my class
  You're in my class .

3 they / late
  _____ .

4 Carmen / in room 4
  _____ .

5 I / class A
  _____ .

6 we / from Mexico
  _____ .

7 They / in Vietnam
  _____ .

8 you / a teacher
  _____ .

b Complete the sentences with the negative ⊟ of *be*.

1 No, I'*m not* from Peru.
2 No, Mary *isn't* a teacher.
3 No, we _____ late.
4 No, Dan _____ English.
5 No, Tokyo _____ in China.
6 No, they _____ Chilean.
7 No, you _____ in my class.
8 No, I _____ Brazilian.

c Order the words to make questions.

1 in / 8 / we / Are / room
   Are we in room 8 ?
2 from / Where's / he
   Where's he from ?
3 class / in / 1 / Are / they
   _____ ?
4 from / Where / you / are
   _____ ?
5 they / England / from / Are
   _____ ?
6 Brazilian / Fernanda / Is
   _____ ?
7 in / Seoul / Is / South Korea
   _____ ?
8 name / your / What's
   _____ ?

d Match the answers to the questions in **c**.

a Yes, she is.   _____
b No, they're in class 2. _____
c He's from Portugal.   _2_
d It's Jessica.   _____
e Yes, we are.   _1_
f Yes, it is.   _____
g Yes, they're from London. _____
h I'm from Hanoi in Vietnam. _____

3 PRONUNCIATION word stress; /ʃ/ and /tʃ/

a Underline the stressed syllable. Which word is different? Circle it.

1 tea|cher   (ex|cuse)   Bri|tish   sorr|y
2 Bra|zil   co|ffee   ho|tel   good|bye
3 Bri|tish   Pe|ru   mu|sic   Spa|nish
4 Ja|pan   pho|to   Sau|di   Thurs|day
5 good|bye   En|glish   he|llo   Chi|nese
6 Mex|i|can   Ca|na|da   Vi|et|nam Sa|tur|day

b 🔲iChecker Listen and check. Then listen again and repeat the words.

c Write the words in the chart.

British	chair	China	dictionary
Portugal	Spanish	teacher	vacation

∫ shower	t∫ chess
British _____	_____ _____
_____ _____	_____ _____

d 🔲iChecker Listen and check. Then listen again and repeat the words.

4 LISTENING

a 🔲iChecker Listen and number the pictures 1–3.

A    B

C

b 🔲iChecker Listen again. Write the nationalities.

1 The man is _____ .
2 Pho is _____ .
3 The members of Coldplay are _____ .

USEFUL WORDS AND PHRASES

Learn these words and phrases.

seat   /siːt/
free   /friː/
Thanks! /θæŋks/
please   /pliːz/
on vacation   /ɒn veɪˈkeɪʃn/
student   /ˈstjuːdnt/
and   /ænd/
too   /tuː/

One in ten people would prefer to lose their
mother-in-law than their cell phone.

From a 2006 poll of Canadians

2B What's his number?

1 VOCABULARY numbers 11–100; personal information

a Complete the numbers.

1 **20** t we nt y
2 **15** f___t___n
3 **90** ni___t__
4 **70** s__v__nt__
5 **12** t___lv__
6 **100** a hu___r___

7 **80** ei___t__
8 **11** e___v__
9 **40** fo__t__
10 **13** th__r___n
11 **60** si__t__

b Write the numbers.

1 forty-seven   _47_
2 nineteen   _____
3 thirty-eight   _____
4 fifty-nine   _____
5 seventy-two   _____
6 fourteen   _____
7 ninety-one   _____
8 sixteen   _____
9 twenty-three   _____
10 eighteen   _____

c Match the questions and answers.

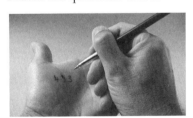

1 What's your phone number?   _c_
2 What's your zip code?   ___
3 Are you single?   ___
4 What's your last name?   ___
5 What's your address?   ___
6 How old are you?   ___
7 What's your email?   ___
8 How do you spell your last name?   ___

a It's Ferreira.
b F-E-R-R-E-I-R-A.
c It's 493-555-3908.
d I'm 27.
e 90180.
f No, I'm not. I'm married.
g It's 603 Green Street.
h bortega@aefmail.com.

2 GRAMMAR Wh- and How questions with be

a Complete the questions. Write one word in each blank.

1 A _Who_ _is_ Sarah Lawson?
  B She's my English teacher.
2 A _____ _____ the concert?
  B It's on Monday.
3 A Where _____ _____ from?
  B She's from Spain.
4 A _____ _____ you?
  B I'm good, thanks. And you?
5 A _____ _____ your phone number?
  B It's 818-555-9284.
6 A _____ _____ you from?
  B I'm from Brazil.
7 A _____ _____ Mari and Laura today?
  B They're on vacation in Boston.
8 A _____ _____ Pedro?
  B He's 27.
9 A _____ _____ your address?
  B It's 47 Bank Street.

b Complete the conversation. Write the questions.

A ¹ _What's your name?_
B My name's Brian Halley.
A ² _____?
B H-A-L-L-E-Y.
A Thank you. ³ _____
  _____?
B It's 64 Bond Street, New York City.
A ⁴ _____?
B 10012.
A Thank you. ⁵ _____?
B My home phone number is 784-2913.
A ⁶ _____?
B My cell phone number is 203-555-8479.
A ⁷ _____?
B It's b.halley@gomail.com.
A Thank you. ⁸ _____?
B I'm 23.
A ⁹ _____?
B No, I'm not. I'm single.

c **iChecker** Listen and check. Then listen again and repeat the conversation.

3 PRONUNCIATION saying phone numbers; sentence stress

a Say the phone numbers. Make your voice go up and down.

1 989-220-7415

2 347-680-2919

3 234-571-8001

4 510-659-3374

5 493-743-6515

6 652-802-9450

b **iChecker** Listen and check. Then listen again and repeat the phone numbers.

c **iChecker** Listen and repeat the questions. Stress the **bold** words.

1 **What's** your **cell phone number**?

2 **How old** is **Kim**?

3 **What's** your **email address**?

4 Are you **married**?

5 **What's** your **address**?

6 **How** do you **spell** your **last name**?

4 LISTENING

iChecker Listen to the dialogues. Circle the right answer.

1 What is his address?
a 38 Lake Street   b 48 Lake Street

2 What is her cell phone number?
a 203-868-5174   b 203-868-5144

3 What is his first name?
a S-H-U-H-A-O   b S-H-U-H-O-W

4 What is his zip code?
a 12305   b 12345

USEFUL WORDS AND PHRASES

Learn these words and phrases.

address   /'ædrɛs/

email address   /'imeɪl 'ædrɛs/

home phone number   /hoʊm foʊn 'nʌmbər/

cell phone number   /sɛl foʊn 'nʌmbər/

zip code   /zɪp koʊd/

married   /'mærid/

single   /'sɪŋgl/

lost   /lɔst/

or   /ɔr/

OK   /oʊ'keɪ/

Right.   /raɪt/

Really?   /'rili/

3A What's in your bag?

VOCABULARY small things

Complete the crossword.

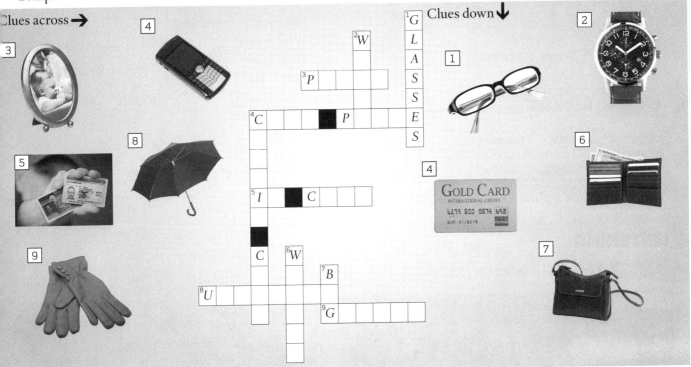

Clues across →

Clues down ↓

2 GRAMMAR *a/an*; singular and plural nouns

a Write *a* or *an*.

1 *a* camera
2 *an* umbrella
3 ____ book
4 ____ watch
5 ____ laptop
6 ____ country
7 ____ ID card
8 ____ key
9 ____ wallet
10 ____ email

b Write the plurals of the words in **a**.

1 *cameras*
2 ____
3 ____
4 ____
5 ____
6 ____
7 ____
8 ____
9 ____
10 ____

c Write questions and answers.

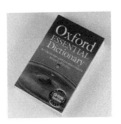   

1 *What is it*____?
   It's a dictionary.

2 *What are they*?
   They're gloves.

3 _____?
   _____.

4 _____?
   _____.

5 _____?
   _____.

6 _____?
   _____.

7 _____?
   _____.

8 _____?
   _____.

3 PRONUNCIATION /z/ and /s/; plural endings

a **iChecker** Listen and repeat the words and sounds.

zebra	1 nam**es**	bag**s**
snake	2 book**s**	student**s**
/ɪz/	3 bus**es**	class**es**

b **iChecker** Listen and circle two more words with /ɪz/.

cell phones	coats	(glasses)
gloves	ID cards	laptops
pieces	wallets	watches

c **iChecker** Listen again and repeat the words.

b **iChecker** Listen again. Complete the questions.

1 **A** Look. They're great.
   B Yes, they are. But, uh, **w**_____ _____ _____?
2 Excuse me, ma'am. **W**_____ _____ your _____?
3 Is it for me? Thanks! **W**_____ _____ _____?

USEFUL WORDS AND PHRASES

Learn these words and phrases.

What is it? /wʌt ɪz ɪt/
What are they? /wʌt ɑr ðeɪ/
Have /hæv/
leave /liv/
miss /mɪs/
ma'am /mæm/
sir /sər/
great /greɪt/
Happy birthday! /ˈhæpi ˈbərθdeɪ/

---

4 LISTENING

a **iChecker** Listen and number the pictures 1–3.

A hat should be taken off when you greet a lady and left off for the rest of your life. Nothing looks more stupid than a hat.

P. J. O'Rourke, American journalist and author

VOCABULARY more small things

Complete the crossword.

Clues across ➡   Clues down ⬇

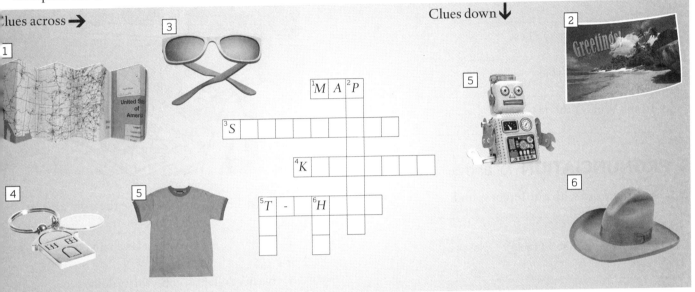

GRAMMAR this / that / these / those

Complete the sentences with *this, that, these,* or *those*.

1 *Those* are $10.

2 **A** Is _____ a good hat?
   B No, it isn't.

3 _____ isn't a toy!

4 **A** Are _____ your keys?
   B Yes, they are. Thank you!

5 Look! _____'s Martin from English class.

6 Wow. _____ are good sunglasses!

b Order the words to make sentences or questions.

1 these / sunglasses / Are

 Are these sunglasses ?

2 is / What / that

 _____ ?

3 book / isn't / This / your

 _____ .

4 postcards / my / Those / are

 _____ .

5 your / Are / gloves / those

 _____ ?

6 my / aren't / photos / These

 _____ .

7 that / friend / Is / your

 _____ ?

8 from / Where / this / is

 _____ ?

3 PRONUNCIATION /ð/ and /æ/

a Circle the word with a different sound.

æ cat	1 hat	(table)	glasses
æ cat	2 card	laptop	camera
ð mother	3 **th**ese	**th**ose	d**a**y
æ cat	4 Sp**ai**n	Sp**a**nish	C**a**nada
æ cat	5 b**a**g	m**a**p	b**a**by

b **iChecker** Listen and check. Then listen again and repeat the words.

4 LISTENING

a **iChecker** Listen and number the items 1–4.

b **iChecker** Listen again. Choose the right answer.

1 It's _____ .
  a a toy   b a keychain
2 It's _____ .
  a twenty dollars b thirty dollars
3 They're _____ .
  a two dollars   b good
4 They're _____ .
  a seven dollars b ten dollars

USEFUL WORDS AND PHRASES

Learn these words and phrases.

cute /kyut/
That's a lot. /ðæts ə lɑt/
I'm <u>sorry</u>. /aɪm ˈsɑri/
Is this your…? /ɪz ðɪs yɔr/
How a<u>bout</u>…? /haʊ əˈbaʊt/
for sale /fɔr seɪl/
map of the <u>city</u> /mæp əv ðə ˈsɪti/

PRICES

Complete the prices.

1 $0.75   seventy-five _cents_
2 £21.99   twenty-one _____ ninety-nine
3 $38.50   thirty-eight _____ and fifty cents
4 40p   forty _____
5 €11.60   eleven _____ sixty
6 $1.82   a _____ eighty-two

Write the prices.

1 _forty-five cents_

2 _____

3 _____

4 _____

5 _____

6 _____

7 _____

8 _____

PRONUNCIATION /ʊr/, /s/, and /k/

iChecker Listen and repeat the words and sounds.

ʊr tourist	1 **sure** **eur**o **tour**

S snake	2 ni**ce** pri**ce** **c**ell phone
k key	3 **c**lass **c**redit **c**ard **C**anada

b Write the words in the chart.

city   **c**ute   **c**ent   **c**lose   **c**offee   pen**ce**

S snake	**k** key
city	_cute_
_____	_____
_____	_____

c **iChecker** Listen and check. Then listen again and repeat the words.

3 BUYING A COFFEE

Order the dialogue.

Waitress
____ Six dollars and twenty cents, please.
____ What kind of coffee? Espresso, cappuccino, or latte?
_1_   Welcome to Coffee House.
____ Thanks. Here's your change.
____ Regular or large?

Man
____ A latte, please.
_2_   Hi. A coffee and a cookie, please.
____ Here you are.
____ Large. How much is it?

4A Family and friends

1 VOCABULARY people and family

a Complete the chart.

singular	plural
boy	¹*boys*
²	girls
woman	³
man	⁴
⁵	friends
child	⁶
person	⁷

b Complete the sentences.

1 Max's my **f***ather*_____ .
2 Peter's my **h**_____ .
3 Barbara's my **m**_____ .
4 Lily's my **d**_____ .
5 Rob's my **br**_____ .
6 Jaden's my **s**_____ .
7 Lucy's my **s**_____ .
8 I'm Peter's **w**_____ .

2 GRAMMAR possessive adjectives; possessive *s*

a Complete the chart.

I	¹*my*
²*you*	your
he	³
⁴	her
it	⁵
⁶	our
you	⁷
⁸	their

b Complete the sentences.

1 That's _____*my*_____ laptop!

2 Here's _____ coffee, sir.

3 What's _____ name?

4 Look at _____ hat.

5 _____ children are cute!

6 This is _____ house.

7 That's _____ toy.

8 _____ car is great!

Complete the sentences.

1 Carmen is Diego's sister.
   Diego is ___Carmen's brother_____.
2 Charlotte is Peter's wife.
   Peter is _____.
3 Mark is Angelina's brother.
   Angelina is _____.
4 Richard is Maria's father.
   Maria is _____.
5 Ana is Paulo's mother.
   Paulo is _____.
6 William is Megan's husband.
   Megan is _____.
7 Sarah is Michael's daughter.
   Michael is _____.
8 Roberto is Luisa's son.
   Luisa is _____.

Look at the 's in the sentences. Check (✔) Possessive or Is.

		Possessive	Is
1	Mark's wife is Brazilian.	✔	☐
2	Tiffany's on vacation.	☐	✔
3	Those are Amy's cats.	☐	☐
4	It's a great cell phone.	☐	☐
5	This is my brother's room.	☐	☐
6	Jennifer's in Brazil.	☐	☐
7	What's your name?	☐	☐
8	Peter's son is twelve.	☐	☐

PRONUNCIATION /ə/, /ʌ/, and /ər/

Circle the word with a different sound.

arrow	1	(camera)	umbrella	gloves
arrow	2	mother	husband	person
computer	3	woman	son	children
arrow	4	Sunday	Monday	Thursday

iChecker Listen and check. Then listen again and repeat the words.

Circle the words with /ər/.

1	morning	(person)	Arabic
2	understand	camera	card
3	chair	paper	door
4	zero	four	thirty

d iChecker Listen and check. Then listen again and repeat the words.

4 LISTENING

a iChecker Listen and number the pictures 1–4.

b iChecker Listen again. Choose a or b.

1 The girl is the man's _____ .
   a sister   b sister's daughter
2 The woman in the picture is Tom's _____.
   a teacher   b girlfriend
3 The woman's phone is _____ .
   a in her bag   b on the chair
4 Mia's last name is _____ .
   a Lee   b Cho

USEFUL WORDS AND PHRASES

Learn these words and phrases.

Welcome to our house. /ˈwɛlkəm tu ɑr haʊs/
babysitter /ˈbeɪbɪsɪtər/
Be nice. /bi naɪs/
have /hæv/
on /ɑn/
Oh. /oʊ/
Uh-oh. /ˈʌ oʊ/

4B That's a cool car!

1 VOCABULARY colors and common adjectives

a Rewrite the sentences with a color.

1 My car is D E R.
   _My car is red_____.

2 Amelia's coat is C A B L K.
   _____.

3 His bag is N O W B R.
   _____.

4 Gabriel's T-shirt is E L U B.
   _____.

5 The board is H E T I W.
   _____.

6 Their house is N E R G E.
   _____.

7 Her gloves are W E Y L O L.
   _____.

8 His hat is O G N R E A.
   _____.

b Complete the sentences with the opposite of the **bold** word.

1 Our car isn't **small**.
   It's _big_____.

2 My car isn't **fast**.
   It's _____.

3 Ana's cell phone isn't **cheap**.
   It's _____.

4 His chair isn't **new**.
   It's _____.

5 Mark's coat isn't **long**.
   It's _____.

6 Their teacher isn't **bad**.
   She's _____.

7 My boyfriend isn't **short**.
   He's _____.

c Complete the words.

1 Your hat is **gr**_eat____!

2 Her husband is very **g**___**l**___

3 Have a **n**_____ day!

4 His girlfriend is **b**_____

5 My cat is very **b**_____.

6 This movie is **t**_____!

2 GRAMMAR adjectives

a Right (✓) or wrong (✗)? Correct the wrong sentences.

1 It's a small car. __✓_____

2 It's a phone cheap. __✗ *It's a cheap phone.*_____

3 He's a father great. _____

4 They're blues pens. _____

5 Their children are talls. _____

6 Tiger is a cute cat. _____

7 He's a man good-looking. _____

8 She's a short woman. _____

Rewrite the sentences.

1 The woman is beautiful.
   She's __*a beautiful woman*__ .
2 The coats are yellow.
   They're __*yellow coats*__ .
3 The people are nice.
   They're _____ .
4 The class is good.
   It's _____ .
5 The hat is black.
   It's _____ .
6 The laptops are cheap.
   They're _____ .
7 The girl is tall.
   She's _____ .
8 The cars are fast.
   They're _____ .

PRONUNCIATION /ɔ/, /ɑr/, and /ɔr/

Circle the words with /ɔ/.

1 (small)   **o**ld   fa**st**
2 slow   goo**d**   long
3 tall   bad   chea**p**
4 mother   dau**gh**ter son

iChecker Listen and check. Then listen again and repeat the words.

Circle the word with a different sound.

ɔr horse	1	board	(car)	door
ɑr car	2	park	**are**	Portugal
ɔr horse	3	ID c**ar**d	**or**ange	sh**or**t
ɑr car	4	M**ar**k	four	**ar**ticle

iChecker Listen and check. Then listen again and repeat the words.

 Listen and check (✓) the correct picture.

1 A ☐   B ☐

2 A ☐   B ☐

3 A ☐   B ☐

USEFUL WORDS AND PHRASES

Learn these words and phrases.

German   /ˈdʒɜrmən/
Italian   /ɪˈtælyən/
cool   /kul/
luxurious   /lʌɡˈʒʊriəs/
easy to park   /ˈizi tu pɑrk/
safe   /seɪf/
important   /ɪmˈpɔrtnt/
popular   /ˈpɑpyələr/
What color is it?   /wʌt ˈkʌlər ɪz ɪt/
Have a nice day!   /hæv ə naɪs deɪ/
Hey!   /heɪ/
Wow!   /waʊ/

Some of the worst mistakes
my life have been haircut▮
Jim Morrison, American rock sing▮

5A A bad hair day

1 GRAMMAR simple present: *I* and *you*

a Complete the sentences. Use each verb once.

~~drink~~	have	like	live	want

1 I _drink_ coffee. ⊞

2 I _____ four children. ⊞

3 I _____ a magazine. ⊟

4 I _____ downtown. ⊞

5 I _____ cats. ⊟

b Write the questions.

1 A I don't live downtown.
   B _Do you live_ _____ near here?
2 A I don't want a newspaper.
   B _____ a magazine?
3 A I don't like dogs.
   B _____ cats?
4 A I don't have a camera.
   B _____ a cell phone?
5 A I don't drink soda.
   B _____ coffee?

c Complete the dialogue with *do* or *don't*.

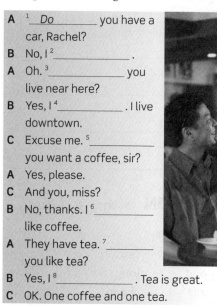

A ¹ _Do_ you have a car, Rachel?
B No, I ² _____ .
A Oh. ³ _____ you live near here?
B Yes, I ⁴ _____ . I live downtown.
C Excuse me. ⁵ _____ you want a coffee, sir?
A Yes, please.
C And you, miss?
B No, thanks. I ⁶ _____ like coffee.
A They have tea. ⁷ _____ you like tea?
B Yes, I ⁸ _____ . Tea is great.
C OK. One coffee and one tea.

d (iChecker) Listen and check. Then listen again and repeat the dialogue.

2 VOCABULARY common verbs 1

Write the verbs.

~~drink~~	eat	have	listen to	read	speak	want	watch

1 I _drink_ soda.
2 I _____ two cats.
3 I _____ TV in the evening.
4 I _____ Chinese.
5 I _____ Mexican food.
6 I _____ magazines.
7 I _____ a new car.
8 I _____ Brazilian music.

READING

Read the interview and write the questions in the correct space.

Are you married?	Do you work near here?
Do you have children?	~~What's your name?~~
Do you like it?	Where are you from?

Interview with
a hairstylist

1 _What's your name?_
   My name's Jonathan, Jon for short.
2 _____
   I'm from Rio de Janeiro. It's a big, beautiful city.
3 _____
   Yes, I am. My wife is Italian. Her name is Celia. She's very good-looking!
4 _____
   Yes, we do. We have a little girl. Her name is Bianca. She's three.
5 _____
   Yes, I do. I work in a salon downtown. It's very small, but it's nice.
6 _____
   Yes, I do. I work with my friends, and I speak to a lot of new people every day. It's very interesting.

b Look at the highlighted words and phrases. What do you think they mean? Check with your dictionary.

PRONUNCIATION /h/, /w/, and /v/; linking

a Circle the word with a different sound.

W witch	1 where	what	(who)
V vase	2 very	want	TV
h house	3 who	white	hair

b **iChecker** Listen and check. Then listen again and repeat the words.

c **iChecker** Listen and repeat. Copy the rhythm.
1 Do you **want** a **soda**?
2 I have a **brother** and he's a **teacher**.
3 I **drink** a **coffee** and **read** a **book** in the **morning**.
4 I **live** in a **house** in a **small city**.

5 LISTENING

iChecker Listen to the dialogues and choose a or b.
1 The woman lives _____ .
   a near here   b downtown
2 The man has _____ children.
   a one   b two
3 The woman _____ TV.
   a likes   b doesn't like
4 The man speaks _____ .
   a Spanish   b Japanese
5 The woman listens to _____ music.
   a pop   b classical

USEFUL WORDS AND PHRASES

Learn these words and phrases.

hair   /hɛr/
hairstylist   /hɛrˈstaɪlɪst/
salon   /səˈlɑn/
first time   /fərst taɪm/
magazine   /mægəˈzin/
near here   /nɪr hɪr/
downtown   /daʊnˈtaʊn/
Don't worry.   /doʊnt ˈwəri/
Wait.   /weɪt/
little   /ˈlɪtl/
a lot of   /ə lɑt əv/

Eat breakfast like a king, lunch li|
a prince, and dinner like a poor ma|

Adelle Davis, nutrition|

1 VOCABULARY food and drink

a Complete the crossword.

Clues down ↓

Clues across →

b What do they have for dinner? Complete the words.

1 f i s h   2 s a l a d   3 t _ a

4 p _ _ _ a   5 v _ _ _ _ _ _ _ s   6 m _ _ k

7 m _ _ t   8 p _ _ _ _ _ s   9 w _ _ _ r

10 a s _ _ _ _ _ _ h 11 c _ _ _ _ _ _ _ e 12 or _ _ _ e j _ _ _ e

2 PRONUNCIATION word stress; /tʃ/, /dʒ/, and /g/

a Underline the stressed syllable.

ty|pi|cal	de|li|cious	te|rri|ble	ex|pen|sive
ham|bur|ger	um|bre|lla	po|ta|toes	
cer|e|al	to|ge|ther	vege|ta|bles	

b iChecker Listen and check. Then listen again and repeat the words.

Circle the word with a different sound.

... girl	1	**g**o	hambur**g**er	(o**r**an**g**e)
chess	2	**ch**eap	**ch**ef	lun**ch**
jazz	3	ve**g**etables	su**g**ar	**j**uice
chess	4	**G**erman	**ch**eese	Por**tu**guese
girl	5	**g**ood	bi**g**	pa**g**e
chess	6	**Ch**inese	**J**apanese	**ch**ildren

d **iChecker** Listen and check. Then listen again and repeat the words.

3 GRAMMAR simple present: *we, you, they*; *Wh-* questions

a Write sentences. Use the verbs from the list.

drink	have	listen to	live
read	~~want~~	watch	~~work~~

1 We / a new car ⊞
   We want a new car .

2 You / work on Saturday ⊟
   You don't work on Saturday .

3 We / magazines ⊞
   _____ .

4 Rodrigo and Ana / pop music ⊟
   _____ .

5 My brother and I / cereal for breakfast ⊞
   _____ .

6 They / TV at dinner ⊟
   _____ .

7 My friends / downtown ⊞
   _____ .

8 My children / coffee ⊟
   _____ .

b Complete the questions.

1 A *Do they live* _____ in Mexico?
   B No, they live in Peru.
2 A _____ children?
   B Yes, we do – a son and two daughters.
3 A _____ for breakfast?
   B They usually have cereal, toast, and juice.
4 A _____ English?
   B Yes, they do. Their English is very good.
5 A _____ lunch?
   B We have lunch at home.
6 A _____ coffee for breakfast?
   B Yes, we do – coffee with milk.
7 A _____ dinner in Spain?
   B People have dinner late in Spain – at 10:00 or 11:00 p.m.
8 A _____ pizza?
   B Yes, we do. We love pizza!
9 A _____ ?
   B They work in a school. They're teachers.
10 A _____ ?
   B We live in an apartment downtown.

4 LISTENING

a **iChecker** Listen and number the pictures 1–4.

A

B

C

D

b **iChecker** Listen again. Choose a or b.

1 The woman likes _____ for breakfast.
   a toast   b pizza
2 The woman eats a big _____ .
   a breakfast   b lunch
3 The man likes _____ .
   a cereal   b fruit
4 The man doesn't like _____ .
   a cheese   b vegetables

USEFUL WORDS AND PHRASES

Learn these words and phrases.

simple /ˈsɪmpl/
typical /ˈtɪpɪkl/
traditional /trəˈdɪʃənl/
usually /ˈyuʒuəli/
cold /koʊld/
I know. /aɪ noʊ/
That's good. /ðæts gʊd/
That looks good. /ðæt lʊks gʊd/

Practical English What time is it?

1 TELLING TIME

a Complete the times.

1 It's two __thirty__ . 2 It's eight _____ .

3 It's ten _____. 4 It's a _____ to six.

5 It's eleven _____. 6 It's twelve _____.

7 It's nine _____. 8 It's _____ to seven.

b Complete the dialogues.

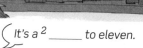

What ¹ _time_ is it?   It's a ² _____ to eleven.

Excuse me. ³ _____ time is it?   Sorry, I don't ⁴ _____ a wate

What time is ⁵ _____ ?   ⁶ _____ a quarter to four.

⁷ _____ me. What time is it?

Sorry. I ⁸ _____ know

6A He speaks English at work

GRAMMAR simple present: *he, she, it*

a Look at the chart and complete the sentences.

	Amy	Luis
live in a big city	✗	✓
like cats	✓	✗
listen to pop music	✓	✗
speak French	✗	✓
drink tea	✗	✓

1 Amy __doesn't live__ in a big city.
2 She _____ cats.
3 She _____ to pop music.
4 She _____ French.
5 She _____ tea.
6 Luis _____ in a big city.
7 He _____ cats.
8 He _____ to pop music.
9 He _____ French.
10 He _____ tea.

b Complete the text.

Ryan is an English teacher in Mexico. He ¹__lives__ (live) in Mexico City, and he ²_____ (work) in a language school there. He ³_____ (not work) on weekends, so Ryan ⁴_____ (go) to see friends in Puebla.

Ryan ⁵_____ (like) Mexico, but he ⁶_____ (not speak) Spanish very well. He ⁷_____ (have) a Spanish class on Sundays, and he ⁸_____ (study) in the morning on the bus. He ⁹_____ (not watch) TV because he ¹⁰_____ (not understand) the shows!

c Complete the dialogue with *do, does, don't,* or *doesn't.*

Kim	Hi, I'm Kim.
Chris	Hello. I'm Chris.
Kim	What ¹ _do_ you do, Chris?
Chris	I'm a lawyer.
Kim	That's great. ²_____ you like your job?
Chris	Yes, I ³_____ .
Kim	⁴_____ you work in the city?
Chris	Yes, I work downtown and I live in an apartment there.
Kim	⁵_____ you live with your family?
Chris	No, I ⁶_____ . My parents have a house in a small town.
Kim	⁷_____ you have brothers and sisters?
Chris	Yes, I have a brother.
Kim	What ⁸_____ he do?
Chris	He's a student.
Kim	⁹_____ he live at home?
Chris	No, he ¹⁰_____ . He lives in an apartment at school.

2 PRONUNCIATION third person –s

a **iChecker** Listen and repeat the words and sounds.

zebra	1 ha**s** read**s**
snake	2 eat**s** speak**s**
/ɪz/	3 clos**es** teach**es**

b Circle three more words with /ɪz/ and write them in the chart.

closes	drinks	finishes	goes	likes
teaches	listens	opens	watches	works

_____

/ɪz/	_closes_ _____ _____
	_____ _____

c **iChecker** Listen and check. Then listen again and repeat the words.

27

3 VOCABULARY jobs and places of work

a Look at the pictures and complete the puzzle. What's the mystery word?

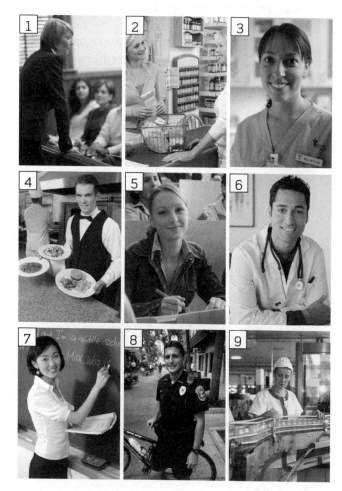

b Complete the sentences with a place of work.

1 A writer works at h*ome* .
2 A factory worker works in a **f**_____ .
3 A salesperson works in a **st**_____ .
4 An assistant works in an **o**_____ .
5 A teacher works in a **sc**_____ .
6 A waitress works in a **r**_____ .
7 A policeman works on the **st**_____ .
8 A nurse works in a **h**_____ .

4 LISTENING

iChecker Listen to the dialogues. What do the peopl do? Do they like their jobs? Complete the chart.

	What do they do?	Do they like it?
1		Yes / No
2		Yes / No
3		Yes / No
4		Yes / No

USEFUL WORDS AND PHRASES

Learn these words and phrases.

fantastic /fæn'tæstɪk/
practice /'præktəs/
company /'kʌmpəni/
tour guide /tʊr gaɪd/
museum /myu'ziəm/
art /ɑrt/
prefer /prɪ'fər/

6B Do you like mornings?

1 VOCABULARY a typical day

Complete the verb phrases.

1 **w** *atch* TV

2 **d**_____ housework

3 **g**_____ to work

4 **h**_____ a sandwich

5 **g**_____ up

6 **m**_____ dinner

7 **g**_____ shopping

8 **g**_____ to bed

b Write the words in the chart.

to-bed	breakfast	a coffee	to the gym	home
lunch	a sandwich	to school	dinner	to work

have	go
breakfast	*to bed*

c Complete the text.

I'm Mike and I'm a factory worker. I work at night and I sleep during the day. I¹ _finish_ work at eight o'clock in the morning, and then I² _____ home and ³ _____ to bed. I⁴ _____ up at about two-thirty in the afternoon, and I⁵ _____ a big breakfast – eggs, potatoes, sausage, and of course a lot of coffee! I⁶ _____ to the gym after breakfast, then I⁷ _____ a shower and I⁸ _____ TV. At seven o'clock in the evening, I⁹ _____ dinner. Then I¹⁰ _____ to work again.

2 PRONUNCIATION sentence stress

iChecker Listen and repeat. <u>Copy</u> the <u>rhythm</u>.

1 I **start work** at **nine** in the **morning**.
2 She has a **coffee** at **quarter** after **ten**.
3 They have a **sandwich** at a **cafe**.
4 You **finish work** at **six-thirty**.
5 We do **housework** on **weekends**.
6 He **watches TV** in the **evening**.

29

3 GRAMMAR adverbs of frequency

a Rewrite the sentences. Use the words in parentheses.

1 I get up early. (always)
   I always get up early .

2 Yasmin goes to school by bus. (usually)
   _____ .

3 You do housework. (never)
   _____ .

4 They have fish for dinner. (sometimes)
   _____ .

5 Andy goes to the gym. (always)
   _____ .

6 I watch TV in the morning. (never)
   _____ .

7 We go shopping on weekends. (sometimes)
   _____ .

8 They have coffee for breakfast. (usually)
   _____ .

b Look at the chart and complete the sentences.

	 Diego	 Jen
go to the gym	✗	✓✓✓✓✓
read magazines	✓	✓✓✓
watch soccer on TV	✓✓✓✓✓	✓
get up early	✓✓✓	✗

✓✓✓✓✓ = always
✓✓✓ = usually
✓ = sometimes
✗ = never

1 Diego __never goes__ to the gym.
2 He _____ magazines.
3 He _____ soccer on TV.
4 He _____ early.
5 Jen _____ to the gym.
6 She _____ magazines.
7 She _____ soccer on TV.
8 She _____ early.

4 LISTENING

a **iChecker** Listen to the interview with Tony. Circle the things he usually or always does on the weekend.

b **iChecker** Listen again. Put an ✗ over the things he never does on the weekend.

USEFUL WORDS AND PHRASES

Learn these words and phrases.

in a <u>hurry</u> /ɪn ə ˈhəri/
<u>sit</u>ting down /ˈsɪtɪŋ daʊn/
<u>stand</u>ing up /ˈstændɪŋ ʌp/
when /wɛn/
then /ðɛn/
<u>af</u>ter /ˈæftər/
be<u>fore</u> /bɪˈfɔr/
next /nɛkst/
a<u>bout</u> /əˈbaʊt/

7A Life at the end of the world

1 GRAMMAR word order in questions

a Write questions. Put the words in parentheses in the correct place.

1 Where is from? (Alberto)
   Where is Alberto from ?

2 How old is? (our teacher)
   _____ ?

3 Where does work? (your brother)
   _____ ?

4 Does speak French? (Emma)
   _____ ?

5 Do have a big family? (you)
   _____ ?

6 Is from Canada? (your girlfriend)
   _____ ?

7 What time does go to work? (Isobel)
   _____ ?

8 Are on vacation? (Tim and Julia)
   _____ ?

b Circle the correct question word.

1 A Where / What / When does your brother live?
  B In São Paulo.

2 A Where / When / What do you usually have for breakfast?
  B Cereal, fruit, and coffee.

3 A How / Who / What do you spell your last name?
  B G-A-R-C-I-A.

4 A What / When / Who do you do housework?
  B On Sunday morning.

5 A How / When / Where do you go to school?
  B By bus.

6 A How / How old / What are your children?
  B Jaden's four and Madison's seven.

7 A What / When / Where do you go to the gym?
  B In the morning, before work.

c Look at the answers. Write the questions.

1 *How old is he* ?
  He's **22**.

2 _____ ?
  We play golf **on Saturday**.

3 _____ ?
  Marisa works **in a hospital**.

4 _____ ?
  My teacher's from **Canada**.

5 _____ ?
  Luis has **meat and potatoes** for dinner.

6 _____ ?
  I go to school **by bus**.

7 _____ ?
  She gets up **at six-thirty**.

8 _____ ?
  I like **pop** music.

2 VOCABULARY common verbs 2

Complete the questions.

1 Do you **pl**ay sp*orts* ?
2 Do you **st**_____ **in**_____ on Monday evenings?
3 Do you **g**_____ ice **sk**_____ in the winter?

4 Do your friends ski or **sn**_____ ?
5 Do you **w**_____ a lot on weekends?

6 Does she **pl**_____ the **p**_____ ?
7 Do a lot of tourists **v**_____ your city?
8 Do you **sw**_____ in the summer?

3 PRONUNCIATION /ɛr/, /ɑ/, /aʊ/, and /y/

a (Circle) the word with a different sound.

ɛr chair	1	where	(we're)	very
a clock	2	golf	water	cat
aʊ owl	3	how	snowboard	housework
ɛr chair	4	here	there	hair
a clock	5	table	watch	restaurant

b **iChecker** Listen and check. Then listen again and repeat the words.

c (Circle) five more words with /y/.

(usually)	your	study	play
use	juice	stay	university
Japan	newspaper	yes	museum

d **iChecker** Listen and check. Then listen again and repeat the words.

4 LISTENING

a **iChecker** Listen to the news report. What do people in the Polar Bear Club do? Choose a, b, or c.

a visit Antarctica in the summer
b swim outside in the winter
c play golf in the snow

b **iChecker** Listen again. Complete the information.
1 The water is _____ degrees.
2 About _____ people are in the club.
3 They do this _____ time a year.
4 John goes to a _____ after he swims.

USEFUL WORDS AND PHRASES

Learn these words and phrases.

dark /dɑrk/
light /laɪt/
far from /fɑr frʌm/
close to /kloʊs tu/
hot /hɑt/
cold /koʊld/
low /loʊ/
high /haɪ/
outside /aʊt'saɪd/
inside /ɪn'saɪd/
summer /'sʌmər/
winter /'wɪntər/
same /seɪm/
different /'dɪfrənt/
actually /'æktʃuəli/

7B You can't park here

GRAMMAR can / can't

Complete the sentences with *You can | can't* and a verb from the list.

drink	eat	listen	park	swim	walk

1 *You can't park* here.   4 _____ coffee here.

2 _____ here.   5 _____ food here.

3 _____ now.   6 _____ to the radio here.

Complete the dialogues. Use *Can*, the word in parentheses, and a verb from the list.

go	have	play	read	sit	watch

1 A ___*Can I have*___ a pen? (I)
   B Yes. Take one.
2 A _____ ice-skating on the lake? (we)
   B No. It's too warm today.
3 A _____ TV? (we)
   B OK. What's on today?
4 A Excuse me. _____ here? (I)
   B Sorry, no. That's my friend's seat.
5 A _____ golf on Saturday? (you)
   B Yes. What time?
6 A Look. It's a postcard from Sarah.
   B Really? _____ it? (I)

2 PRONUNCIATION /æ/ and /ə/; sentence rhythm

a What sound does *can* have in these sentences? Circle the correct picture.

1 Can we take photos?
2 You can swim here.
3 When can we talk?
4 You can't walk here.

b **iChecker** Listen and check. Then listen again and repeat the sentences. Copy the rhythm.

3 VOCABULARY common verbs 2

Look at the pictures and complete the phrases.

1 u*se* the I*nternet*_____   5 ch_____ m_____
2 t_____ ph_____   6 s_____
3 h_____   7 dr_____
4 p_____ by cr_____ c_____   8 co_____

33

4 READING

a Read the text and number the pictures in the correct order.

 A

 B

 C

 D

b Read the text again. Mark the sentences T (True) or F (False).

Life on the International Space Station

Some people dream of going to space. However, life in space is not very easy. Here are some of the problems that people on the International Space Station (ISS) have.

1 Having lunch on the ISS is very difficult because there is no gravity in space, and things never stay where you put them. The food is in plastic containers because it can't stay on a plate.

2 When they go outside, people wear special clothes, because there is no atmosphere in space. It is also very cold in space. Inside the ISS, people can wear ordinary clothes.

3 You can't take a shower in space because the water doesn't stay in one place. People wash with a sponge with water and soap.

4 People on the ISS can't sleep in ordinary beds because their bodies don't stay in the beds. They use special sleeping bags on the wall.

If you want to take a vacation in space, remember that life there is very different from life at home. And if you don't like it, you can't take a train or bus home!

1 You can eat food on a plate. __F__
2 You can eat food from a plastic container. _____
3 You can wear a T-shirt inside the ISS. _____
4 You can take a shower in the ISS. _____
5 You can wash with a sponge. _____
6 You can sleep in an ordinary bed. _____

c Look at the highlighted words. What do you think they mean? Check with your dictionary.

5 LISTENING

iChecker Listen. Chuck is a tourist in New Orleans. What can he do today? Check (✓) Can or Can't.

Tourist information

	Can	Can't
1 play golf	✓	____
2 take a boat trip	____	____
3 go to the art museum	____	____
4 walk in the park	____	____
5 go to the aquarium	____	____
6 buy a ticket here	____	____
7 buy food at the aquarium	____	____
8 buy food here	____	____

USEFUL WORDS AND PHRASES

Learn these words and phrases.

space /speɪs/
gravity /ˈgrævəti/
plate /pleɪt/
clothes /kloʊz/
atmosphere /ˈætməsfɪr/
ordinary /ˈɔrdnɛri/
sponge /spʌndʒ/
sleeping bag /ˈslipɪŋ bæg/
What else? /wʌt ɛls/
open /ˈoʊpən/
closed /kloʊzd/
aquarium /əˈkwɛriəm/

MONTHS

Write the months.

1 C R A H M _____March_____
2 Y M A _____
3 E R R F A B U Y _____
4 T O B O C R E _____
5 U T G A S U _____
6 E M D B E C R E _____
7 N U R A J A Y _____
8 U E N J _____
9 S M E B R E T E P _____
10 P A I L R _____
11 E O N B M E R V _____
12 L U J Y _____

ORDINAL NUMBERS

Complete the ordinal numbers.

1 **2**nd s e c o n d
2 **20**th tw _ _ _ i _ _ _
3 **31**st th _ _ _ _ - f _ _ _ _
4 **5**th f _ f _ _
5 **9**th n _ _ t _
6 **3**rd t _ _ _ _
7 **12**th tw _ _ _ _ h
8 **8**th e _ g _ _ _

Write the next ordinal number.

1 first, _____second_____
2 tenth, _____
3 seventeenth, _____
4 fourteenth, _____
5 twenty-third, _____
6 fifteenth, _____

3 SAYING THE DATE

a Match the dates.

1	2/19	_f_	a	July twenty-first
2	9/2	____	b	November seventh
3	7/21	____	c	January eleventh
4	1/11	____	d	May sixth
5	4/27	____	e	October eighth
6	10/8	____	f	February nineteenth
7	5/6	____	g	April twenty-seventh
8	11/7	____	h	September second

b Cover a–h and just look at 1–8. Practice saying the dates.

c Write the answers.

1 **A** What's the date today? (3/9)
   B _____March ninth_____ .
2 **A** What's the date on Saturday? (11/1)
   B _____ .
3 **A** What's the date tomorrow? (6/2)
   B _____ .
4 **A** When's your friend's birthday? (12/18)
   B _____ .
5 **A** When's Halloween? (10/31)
   B _____ .
6 **A** When's your sister's birthday? (8/4)
   B _____ .

8A What are they doing?

1 GRAMMAR present continuous

a Complete the chart with the *-ing* form of verbs in the list.

drive	watch	run	get	make	play
sit	study	swim	work	use	write

+ *-ing*	e + *-ing*
watching	driving
_____	_____
_____	_____
_____	_____

double consonant + *-ing*	
running	_____
_____	_____

b Complete the sentences with the verbs from exercise **a** in the present continuous.

1 Erica ___*is running*___ at the gym.
2 _____ you _____ the Internet?
3 They _____ in the lake.
4 It's 7:00 a.m. here. I _____ up now.
5 The students _____ down in class.
6 Peter _____ his mother's car.
7 Lisa _____ Spanish.
8 _____ he _____ at the office?
9 They _____ TV at the dinner table.
10 Luis _____ breakfast.
11 _____ Maria _____ an email to her boyfriend?
12 _____ you _____ computer games?

2 PRONUNCIATION /ʊ/, /u/, and /ŋ/

a Write the words under the correct sound.

blue	book	do	food	good
look	new	school	sugar	woman

ʊ	u
book	food
_____	_____
_____	_____
_____	_____
_____	_____

b (iChecker) Listen and check. Then listen again and repeat the words.

c Circle five more words with /ŋ/.

want	morning	change	ice-skating
nice	sandwich	drink	inside
sing	England	listen	long

d (iChecker) Listen and check. Then listen again and repeat the words.

3 VOCABULARY verb phrases

Write the verbs.

1 h _a_ _v_ _e_ a good time

2 s _ _ _ in a tent

3 t _ _ _ a bus

4 e _ _ _ _ a meal

5 c _ _ _ _ bags

6 w _ _ _ a hat

7 m _ _ _ new people

8 p _ _ the bill

LISTENING

iChecker Listen to the phone conversation and choose a or b.

1 What kind of party is Nick having?
   a an office party
   b a family party

2 What is the party for?
   a It's someone's birthday.
   b Someone is moving.

3 What is Nick eating?
   a vegetables and fruit
   b fish and vegetables

4 Why does Nick say, "I'm sorry?"
   a Because Tonya can't come to the party.
   b Because everyone is working today.

b **iChecker** Listen again. Check (✓) the things Nick and his family are doing.

☐ 1 eating grilled meat
☐ 2 making a salad
☐ 3 playing tennis
☐ 4 eating a cake
☐ 5 singing a song
☐ 6 working hard

USEFUL WORDS AND PHRASES

Learn these words and phrases.

<u>neigh</u>borhood /ˈneɪbərhʊd/
view (n.) /vyu/
guide (n.) /ɡaɪd/
guest /ɡɛst/
<u>com</u>fortable /ˈkʌmftərbl/
<u>in</u>door /ˈɪndər/
jet lag /dʒɛt læɡ/
<u>fam</u>ily <u>par</u>ty /ˈfæmli ˈpɑrti/
<u>of</u>fice <u>par</u>ty /ˈɔfəs ˈpɑrti/
<u>every</u>one /ˈɛvriwən/
for<u>get</u> /fərˈɡɛt/

8B Today is different

1 VOCABULARY the weather

Circle the correct weather word.

Business travel today
Weather from around the world

Los Angeles	70°F / 21°C	☀
Seattle	45°F / 7°C	🌧
Toronto	25°F / -4°C	❄
Moscow	-13°F / -25°C	☁
London	43°F / 6°C	☁
Dubai	104°F / 40°C	☀
Beijing	50°F / 10°C	🎐

1 It's **sunny** / **cold** in Los Angeles.
2 It's **hot** / **raining** in Seattle.
3 It's **snowing** / **raining** in Toronto.
4 It's **windy** / **cold** in Moscow.
5 It's **warm** / **cloudy** in London.
6 It's **hot** / **windy** in Dubai.
7 It's **windy** / **raining** in Beijing.

2 GRAMMAR present continuous or simple present?

a Circle the correct form.

I (1) **usually work** / **'m usually working** at an office downtown. Today I (2) **work** / **'m working** at home.

We usually (3) **go** / **is going** to school on Tuesday, but today is different. Our class (4) **visits** / **is visiting** the art museum. We (5) **learn** / **'re learning** about Spanish painters.

We (6) **study** / **'re studying** outside today! We (7) **usually do** / **'re usually doing** our homework in the library. But today is different. We (8) **enjoy** / **'re enjoying** the sunny weather.

Complete the dialogues. Use the present continuous or simple present.

1 A Hi, can you talk right now?
   B Sorry, I can't. I'm making dinner. (make)
2 A _____ you _____ in Rio? (live)
   B Yes, I do. It's a big, beautiful city.
3 A Are you busy right now?
   B No, I _____ (not do) anything special.
4 A What _____ Tom _____ today? (wear)
   B A suit.
5 A _____ you _____ the newspaper now? (read)
   B No, you can have it.
6 A How's Tracy's job?
   B Busy. She _____ late every evening. (work)
7 A What _____ you _____? (play)
   B A new computer game called Blur.
8 A How _____ you _____ to work? (go)
   B Usually by bus.

B PRONUNCIATION /ɔ/, /oʊ/, and /eɪ/

a (Circle) four more words with /eɪ/.

| assistant | bad | factory | (great) | have |
| make | salesperson | stay | teacher | waitress |

b iChecker Listen and check. Then listen again and repeat the words.

c (Circle) the word with a different sound.

saw	1	office	call	(home)
phone	2	snow	lawyer	window
saw	3	small	old	long
phone	4	August	October	November

d iChecker Listen and check. Then listen again and repeat the words.

4 LISTENING

a iChecker Listen to the dialogues. What is each person doing now? Check (✓) the correct picture.

1 Amy

A  B

2 Marcus

A  B

3 Steve

A  B

b iChecker Listen again. Who says these things? Which job are they talking about?

	Person	Job
1 "I work on the street."	_____	_____
2 "It's hard work."	_____	_____
3 "It's very interesting."	_____	_____
4 "It isn't my dream job."	_____	_____

USEFUL WORDS AND PHRASES

Learn these words and phrases.

bed and breakfast /bɛd ænd 'brɛkfəst/
curious /'kyʊriəs/
career /kə'rɪr/
owner /'oʊnər/
dream /drim/
vet's office /vɛts 'ɔfəs/
professional /prə'fɛʃənl/

9A In the jungle in Guatemala

1 VOCABULARY hotels

a Complete the crossword.

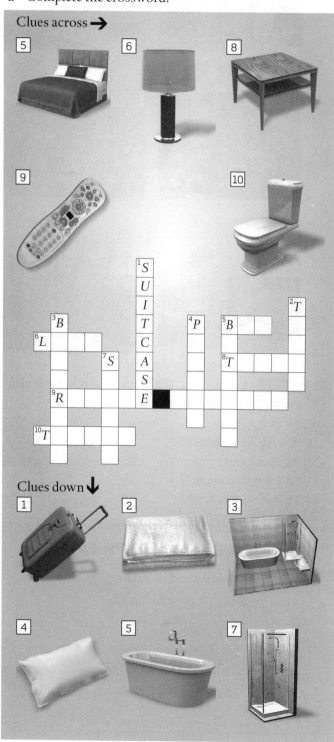

Clues across →

Clues down ↓

1 b Complete the sentences with words from the list.

elevator	gift shop	parking lot	gym
reception	restaurant	swimming pool	yard

1 You can use the ___*elevator*___ to go upstairs.
2 You can swim in the _____ .
3 You can have dinner in the _____ .
4 You can buy a present in the _____ .
5 You can sit outside in the _____ .
6 You can exercise in the _____ .
7 You can park your car in the _____ .
8 You can pay at the _____ .

2 GRAMMAR there's / there are

a Look at the picture. Complete the sentences.

1 ___*There's a*___ bed.
2 ___*There are some*___ pillows.
3 _____ lamp.
4 _____ table.
5 _____ towels.
6 _____ chair.
7 _____ suitcase.
8 _____ books.

b Write negative ⊟ sentences.

1 There's a gym in the hotel. (spa)
   ___*There isn't a spa in the hotel*___ .
2 There are some pillows. (towels)
   ___*There aren't any towels*___ .
3 There are some lamps. (chairs)
   _____ .
4 There's a restaurant in the hotel. (gift shop)
   _____ .

5 There's a swimming pool. (hot tub)

_____ .

6 There are some pens in the room. (books)

_____ .

Write questions and answers.

Welcome to Star Hotel!

Swimming pool	→
Reception	→
Restrooms	→
Elevators	←
Gym	3rd floor
Italian restaurant	5th floor
French restaurant	6th floor

1 restaurants
   Are there any restaurants? Yes, there are.

2 spa
   Is there a spa? No, there isn't.

3 restrooms
   _____

4 swimming pool
   _____

5 gift shops
   _____

6 elevators
   _____

7 gym
   _____

8 hot tub
   _____

PRONUNCIATION /ɛr/, /ɪr/, and /ɔɪ/

a Write the words next to the correct sound.

here	there	airplane	we're	hair
upstairs	wear	year	hear	near

ɛr chair	_there_	___	___	___
	___	___		
ɪr ear	_here_	___	___	___
	___			

b **iChecker** Listen and check. Then listen again and repeat the words.

c Circle three more words with /ɔɪ/.

boyfriend	enj**oy**	five	July
s**ui**tcase	t**oi**let	t**ow**el	t**oy**

d **iChecker** Listen and check. Then listen again and repeat the words.

4 LISTENING

iChecker Listen to the conversation at the hotel reception. Check (✓) Yes or No.

	Yes	No
1 Are there any elevators?	___	✓
2 Is there an ocean view?	___	___
3 Is there a TV in the room?	___	___
4 Are there any books?	___	___
5 Is there a restaurant?	___	___
6 Is there a gym?	___	___
7 Are there any drinks in the room?	___	___
8 Is there a gift shop?	___	___

USEFUL WORDS AND PHRASES

Learn these words and phrases.

modern   /'mɑdərn/
take off   /teɪk ɑf/
land   /lænd/
mattress   /'mætrəs/
present   /'prɛznt/
airplane   /'ɛrpleɪn/
upstairs   /ʌp'stɛrz/
drink (n.)   /drɪŋk/

9B Before they were stars . . .

1 GRAMMAR simple past: *be*

a Rewrite the sentences in the past.

1 I'm at work now.
   I was at work _____ yesterday.
2 They aren't at home today.
   They weren't at home _____ yesterday.
3 He's at a party tonight.
   _____ last night.
4 We aren't at school today.
   _____ yesterday.
5 Are you downtown now?
   _____ last night?
6 She's at the airport this morning.
   _____ yesterday afternoon.
7 Is he late today?
   _____ yesterday?
8 I'm not in a hurry this morning.
   _____ yesterday morning.

b Write questions and answers.

1 Picasso / a painter (✓)
   Was Picasso a painter _____ ?
   Yes, he was _____ .
2 the Beatles / from the United States (✗)
   Were the Beatles from the United States _____ ?
   No, they weren't _____ .
3 Princess Diana / American (✗)
   _____ ?
   _____ .
4 Charles Dickens and Jane Austen / writers (✓)
   _____ ?
   _____ .
5 Carmen Miranda / Brazilian (✓)
   _____ ?
   _____ .
6 Monet and Matisse / singers (✗)
   _____ ?
   _____ .

7 Michael Jackson / a waiter (✗)
   _____
   _____
8 Steve Jobs and Thomas Edison / American (✓)
   _____
   _____

c Complete the dialogues with *was / wasn't*
or *were / weren't*.

1 A ___*Were*___ you at work last week?
  B Yes, I ___*was*___ .
2 A Where _____ you last night?
  B I _____ at a party.
3 A _____ your friend at school yesterday?
  B No, she _____ .
4 A _____ your children on vacation last week?
  B No, they _____ .
5 A When _____ your brother in Boston?
  B He _____ there last year.
6 A _____ you at the museum yesterday?
  B No, we _____ .

2 PRONUNCIATION /ər/ and *was / were*

a What sound do the **bold** words have in these sentences
Circle the correct picture.

1 Where **were** you?

2 She **wasn't** an actress.

3 **Were** they in Boston?

4 Yes, they **were**.

5 **Was** she at school?

6 No, she **wasn't**.

b **iChecker** Listen and check. Then listen again and
repeat the sentences.

3 READING

a Read the text. Mark the sentences T (True) or F (False).

1 Vincent van Gogh was famous during his life.   _F_
2 Vincent was from Germany.   _____
3 Theo van Gogh was Vincent's father.   _____
4 Vincent was a good student.   _____
5 Vincent was a happy person.   _____
6 Vincent's paintings weren't popular in his life.   _____

A FAMOUS PAINTER

Today the artist Vincent van Gogh is very famous, but he was never famous during his life.

Vincent was Dutch. His family was from a small village in the Netherlands. His brother, Theo, was a very important person in his life. Vincent was usually poor, but his brother was always there to help him.

Vincent was interested in school, but he wasn't a very good student. He was always good at painting, but he wasn't a painter at first. He was a teacher and an assistant in a bookstore. After the age of 27, painting was his only job, but he wasn't successful. He was never really happy, and he was often sick. When he was only 37, he ended his life.

When Vincent was alive, he wasn't famous and his paintings weren't popular. Today his pictures are very expensive, and you can see them in museums all over the world.

b Look at the highlighted words. What do you think they mean? Check with your dictionary.

4 VOCABULARY in, at, on: places

Where were these people yesterday? Write sentences with *in*, *at*, or *on* and a word from the list.

train	street	work	boat	beach	the park

1   _She was on the train_   .   2 _____ .

3 _____ .   4 _____ .

5 _____ .   6 _____ .

5 LISTENING

iChecker Listen to the conversations. Choose a or b.

1 A famous person was at the _____ .
  a   gym   b   supermarket
2 The woman was on vacation _____ .
  a   at the beach   b   in the mountains
3 James was _____ yesterday.
  a   in school   b   at the movie theater
4 The man was in Paris _____ .
  a   for work   b   on vacation

USEFUL WORDS AND PHRASES

Learn these words and phrases.

painter   /ˈpeɪntər/
artist   /ˈɑrtɪst/
village   /ˈvɪlɪdʒ/
poor   /pɔr/
successful   /səkˈsɛsfl/
sick   /sɪk/
alive   /əˈlaɪv/
popular   /ˈpɑpyələr/
lucky   /ˈlʌki/
clean   /klin/

43

Practical English Is there a bank near here

1 ASKING WHERE PLACES ARE

Look at the map and answer the questions.

1 Where's the park?
It's _on the corner_ of Park Road and Main Street.
2 Where's the Mexican restaurant?
It's _____ the pharmacy and the museum.
3 Where's the hotel?
It's _____ the bookstore.
4 Where's the movie theater?
It's _____ the bank.
5 Where's the train station?
It's _____ Main Street and Station Road.
6 Where's the bookstore?
It's _____ the museum and the Italian restaurant.
7 Where's the hospital?
It's _____ the pharmacy.

2 ASKING FOR AND GIVING DIRECTIONS

a Look at the map. The people are at the hotel (☆). Complete the places and directions.

1 A Excuse me. Where's the _train station_ ?
B Turn right, go straight ahead, and it's on the _right_
2 A Excuse me. Where's the post office?
B Turn right, and go straight ahead, and then turn _____ . Go _____ ahead, and it's on the _____ , next to the school.
3 A Excuse me. Where's the park?
B Turn right, and go straight _____ , and then turn _____ . Go straight ahead, and it's on the _____ , on the _____ of Park and Main.
4 A Excuse me. Where's the _____ ?
B Turn right, go straight ahead, and it's on the _____ , across from the train station.
5 A Excuse me. Where's the bank?
B Turn left, and go straight ahead, and then turn _____ . Turn _____ again, and it's on the _____ , next to the movie theater.

b iChecker Listen and check your answers. Then listen again and repeat the dialogues.

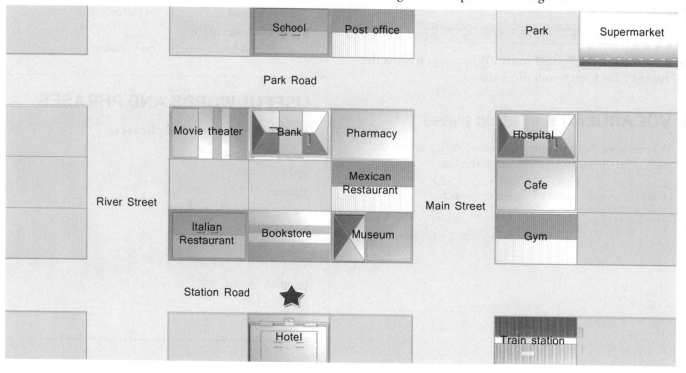

Only I can change my life. No one can do it for me.

Carol Burnett, American actress

10A It changed my life

1 GRAMMAR simple past: regular verbs

Complete the sentences with the simple past of the verbs.

1 We _walked_ in the park on Sunday. (walk)

2 They _____ in Hawaii yesterday morning. (arrive)

3 Lisa _____ work early today. (start)

4 The car _____ at the red light. (stop)

5 Cara _____ a lot during the movie. (cry)

6 April _____ the fish. (like)

b Write negative ☐ sentences using the words in parentheses.

1 Robert talked to Bill. (Tony)
   Robert didn't talk to Tony.

2 Clara arrived this morning. (last night)
   _____.

3 They opened the door. (the window)
   _____.

4 John looked at his phone. (his watch)
   _____.

5 We traveled by bus. (taxi)
   _____.

6 The movie started at 8:20. (7:50)
   _____.

7 Max cooked fish for dinner. (meat)
   _____.

8 Selena learned how to say hello. (goodbye)
   _____.

c Order the words to make questions.

1 learn / Where / you / French / did
   Where did you learn French?

2 you / school / Did / to / walk
   _____?

3 in Brazil / you / did / When / arrive
   _____?

4 greet / How / the teacher / they / did
   _____?

5 the / door / Did / close / Joe
   _____?

6 in school / What / learn / you / did / yesterday
   _____?

7 they / to / talk / Did / the teacher
   _____?

8 start/ your class / What time / did
   _____?

2 VOCABULARY common verbs 3

Complete the questions with the verbs.

arrive	cook	greet	help	laugh
like	miss	move	travel	try

1 Do you _cook_ meals at home every day?

2 Did you _____ to a new house this year?

3 How do you _____ your friends?

4 What time did you _____ ?

5 Did you _____ at the movie?

6 Do you _____ soccer?

7 Do you _____ to school by motorcycle?

8 Does she _____ her baby?

9 Did you _____ anyone yesterday?

10 How often do you _____ new food?

3 PRONUNCIATION regular simple past endings

a iChecker Listen and repeat the words. Practice saying the simple past endings.

d	t	/ɪd/
dog	T-shirt	
learn**ed**	cook**ed**	visit**ed**
mov**ed**	stopp**ed**	start**ed**
travel**ed**	laugh**ed**	end**ed**

b Circle two more simple past forms where -ed is pronounced /ɪd/.

asked	finished	liked	listened	looked	(needed)
played	started	talked	used	wanted	worked

c iChecker Listen and check. Then listen again and repeat the words.

4 LISTENING

iChecker Sam studied in Nepal last year. Listen to an interview with Sam and choose a or b.

1 He lived _____ .
   a in a hotel
   b with a host family
2 He studied _____ .
   a Nepali language and customs
   b Nepali language and history
3 He learned about _____ .
   a Nepali songs
   b Nepali art
4 He traveled to school _____ .
   a on foot
   b by motorcycle
5 He visited _____ .
   a a lake
   b the mountains
6 He tried _____ .
   a Nepali pizza
   b a drink with fruit and yogurt

USEFUL WORDS AND PHRASES

Learn these words and phrases.

on foot /ɒn fʊt/
yogurt /ˈyoʊɡərt/
terrible /ˈtɛrəbl/
delicious /dɪˈlɪʃəs/
terrifying /ˈtɛrəfaɪŋ/
friendly /ˈfrɛndli/

10B What did you do?

VOCABULARY daily routine verbs

Complete the sentences with *do, get, go,* or *have*. Put the verb in the correct form.

1 They always _get_ up early.

2 They _____ to the gym in the morning.

3 She _____ a coffee at about 10:30.

4 They sometimes _____ dinner at a restaurant.

5 They never _____ to bed before 12:00.

6 In the evening, they _____ housework.

7 He usually _____ to work at 8:00 in the morning.

2 GRAMMAR simple past: *do, get, go, have*

a Complete the paragraph with the simple past of *do, get, go,* or *have*.

Yesterday I ¹ _got_ up early, ² _____ a coffee, and ³ _____ to the gym. After the gym, I ⁴ _____ breakfast and ⁵ _____ to work by bus. For lunch, I ⁶ _____ a sandwich with a friend. After work, I ⁷ _____ shopping at the supermarket, then I ⁸ _____ home. I ⁹ _____ dinner with my family, then my wife and I ¹⁰ _____ housework. After that, I ¹¹ _____ to bed early. I was tired!

b Write negative sentences or questions.

1 I went to a movie on Friday. [−]
   I didn't go to a movie on Friday.
2 Isobel had lunch with Tony. [?]
   Did Isobel have lunch with Tony?
3 Marisa did housework on Sunday. [−]
   _____
4 You got up late this morning. [?]
   _____
5 I had breakfast today. [−]
   _____
6 Alison got up early yesterday. [−]
   _____
7 You did your homework last night. [?]
   _____
8 Peter went to the gym on Tuesday. [?]
   _____

c Complete the questions and answers.

1 A What _did_ you _have_ for lunch today?
   B I _____ a sandwich and a salad.
2 A _____ you _____ to the gym after work?
   B No, I _____ . I _____ dinner with a friend, then I _____ home.
3 A What time _____ Tim _____ home yesterday?
   B He _____ home late, about 8:30 or 9:00.
4 A _____ Kim _____ her homework?
   B Yes, she _____ . She _____ her homework on the bus this morning.
5 A What _____ you _____ on the weekend?
   B Nothing special. I _____ up late, I _____ to the gym, and I _____ housework.
6 A _____ your son _____ up early yesterday?
   B No, he _____ . He _____ up at 1:00 p.m.!

3 PRONUNCIATION sentence stress

iChecker Listen and repeat. Copy the <u>rhythm</u>.

1 **What time** did you **get up** this **morning**?
2 Did you **go** to the **gym today**?
3 **Who** did you **have lunch** with?
4 **When** did you **do housework**?
5 Did your **friend have dinner** with you?
6 **Where** did you **go shopping**?

4 READING

a Jessica is an artist in New York City. Read a blog about her day and complete it with the correct form of the verbs.

MY LIFE IN A DAY

People always say, "You're an artist. That's interesting! What do you do all day?"

Yesterday was a typical day for me. What ¹ _did_ I ² _do_ ? (do) First, I ³ _____ (get) up very early, around 6:30. I need a lot of light to paint, and the light is great in the morning. I ⁴ _____ (have) a coffee, but I ⁵ _____ (not have) breakfast. At about 7:30, I ⁶ _____ (go) to work. I have a studio near my house. A lot of artists work there.

After a few hours of work, I ⁷ _____ (get) hungry. I ⁸ _____ (have) a croissant, some fruit, and another coffee. Around 12:00, I ⁹ _____ (go) to my friend's studio and we ¹⁰ _____ (have) lunch together at a cafe.

After lunch, I ¹¹ _____ (go) to the park. I love the flowers there. In the park, I ¹² _____ (get) an idea for a new painting so I ¹³ _____ (go) to the studio again!

I finally ¹⁴ _____ (go) home at about 8:00 in the evening. I ¹⁵ _____ (have) dinner and I ¹⁶ _____ (do) housework. I ¹⁷ _____ (go) to bed around 10:00. I was very tired!

b Read the blog again and number the pictures in order from 1–4.

A
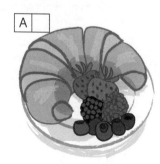

B

C

D

c Look at the highlighted words. What do you think they mean? Check with your dictionary.

5 LISTENING

a **iChecker** Listen to Helena and her husband Steve. Circle *Helena* or *Steve*.

1 Who had a good day?
Helena / Steve
2 Who had a bad day?
Helena / Steve

b **iChecker** Listen again. Write *Helena* or *Steve*.

1 _____ didn't go to an important meeting.
2 _____ had lunch at a nice restaurant.
3 _____ didn't have lunch.
4 _____ finished work very late.
5 _____ got a message.
6 _____ cooked soup.

USEFUL WORDS AND PHRASES

Learn these words and phrases.

need	/nid/	<u>fi</u>nally	/ˈfaɪnli/
<u>stu</u>dio	/ˈstudioʊ/	im<u>por</u>tant	/ɪmˈpɔrtnt/
<u>hun</u>gry	/ˈhʌŋgri/	call	/kɔl/
<u>flow</u>ers	/ˈflaʊərz/	<u>me</u>ssage	/ˈmɛsɪdʒ/
i<u>de</u>a	/aɪˈdiə/		

1A What do you think of it?

GRAMMAR object pronouns: *me, him,* etc.

Complete the sentences with an object pronoun.

1 That's **Ms. Jones**. Do you know ___her___?
2 **Paul** loves his wife and she loves _____ .
3 **I** often call Rob but he never calls _____ .
4 We visited **Chicago** and we loved _____ .
5 I have **glasses** but I never wear _____ .
6 Can **you** hear me? I can hear _____ .
7 I don't usually see **my sister** during the week, but I saw _____ yesterday.
8 **My brother and I** visit our parents every month, but they never visit _____ .

Complete the dialogue. Circle the correct word.

A Do you like Enrique Iglesias, Emma?
B No, I don't like ¹**it** /**him**. And you?
A ²**He's** / **It's** OK.
B What do you think of Shakira?
A I really like ³**her** / **she**. What about you?
B I ⁴**love** / **love her**. ⁵**She's** / **Her** great.
A OK, what about groups? Do you like The Black Eyed Peas?
B ⁶**They're** / **It's** OK.
B I ⁷**don't like** / **don't like them**. ⁸**Them** / **They're** terrible!

2 VOCABULARY opinion words

Complete the sentences with opinion words.

1

2

3

4

5

6

7

1 I love Justin Timberlake. He's **gr**_eat_____ !
2 Justin Beiber is **aw**_____ . I don't like him.
3 Amy MacDonald is **p**_____**y** good. I like her.
4 U2 is OK. They're **n**_____ **b**_____ .
5 Radiohead is great! I **r**_____**y** like them.
6 Katy Perry is **f**_____**c**! I love her.
7 I **c**_____ **st**_____ Lady Gaga. She's terrible.

49

3 READING

a Read the article and mark the sentences T (True) or F (False).

1 Will Champion plays the guitar.   _F_
2 The band started in university.   _____
3 They changed their name in 1996.   _____
4 Their first album wasn't popular.   _____
5 Their second album won a Grammy.   _____
6 X&Y didn't win any Grammy awards.   _____
7 The band doesn't sell a lot of albums.   _____

COLDPLAY

The members of Coldplay are from Britain. The singer is Chris Martin. Jonny Buckland plays the guitar, Guy Berryman plays the bass guitar, and Will Champion plays the drums.

Chris Martin and Jonny Buckland started the band in 1996 when they were students at a university in London. At first their name was Pectoralz, then Starfish, but they changed it to Coldplay in 1997. They became famous in 2000 with the song "Yellow." Their first album, *Parachutes*, won a Grammy in 2002.

Their second album, *A Rush of Blood to the Head*, won a Grammy in 2003. The song "Clocks" also won a Grammy in 2004. They made three more albums: *X&Y* in 2005, *Viva la Vida* in 2008, and *Mylo Xyloto* in 2011. *Viva la Vida* won three Grammy awards.

Coldplay has sold more than 55 million albums. They are famous all over the world and you can hear their songs on the radio almost every day.

b Look at the highlighted words. What do you think they mean? Check with your dictionary.

4 PRONUNCIATION strong stress

iChecker Listen and repeat the dialogues. Give extra stress to the **bold** words.

1 A Listen to this. Do you like it?
  B I **love** it. It's **fantastic**!
  A Yeah. I **love** it.
2 A What do you think of Katy Perry?
  B I can't **stand** her. She's **awful**.
  A Really? I think she's **great**.

5 LISTENING

a **iChecker** Gia and Rob are singers in a pop music group. Listen to the interview. Check (✓) the music Gia likes.

	Gia	Rob
1 Lady Gaga	✓	
2 U2		✓
3 Bono		
4 rock music		
5 hip hop music		
6 The Black Eyed Peas		

b **iChecker** Listen again and check (✓) the music Rob likes.

USEFUL WORDS AND PHRASES

Learn these words and phrases.

guitar   /gɪˈtɑɪ/
bass guitar   /beɪs gɪˈtɑɪ/
drums   /drʌms/
song   /sɒŋ/
album   /ˈælbəm/
award   /əˈwɔrd/

Eat and drink with your relatives; do business with strangers.

Greek proverb

1B Strangers on a train

VOCABULARY common verbs 3

Write the verbs.

1 **t**_urn_ **o**_n_ the light

2 **l**_____ the house

3 **g**_____ a present

4 **g**_____ a letter

5 **l**_____ your keys

6 **w**_____ for the train

7 **t**_____ a story

8 **s**_____ an email

9 **c**_____ a friend

10 **t**_____ an umbrella

2 GRAMMAR simple past: more irregular verbs

Write the past tense.

1	buy	*bought*
2	drive	_____
3	find	_____
4	give	_____
5	leave	_____
6	say	_____
7	see	_____
8	send	_____
9	sit	_____
10	tell	_____
11	think	_____

3 VOCABULARY irregular verbs

a Complete the sentences with the past form of the verbs in parentheses.

1 I __said__ hello to my friend in the street yesterday. (say)

2 Luis _____ a new suit last week. (buy)

3 We _____ to the beach for vacation. (drive)

4 Paula _____ work early today. (leave)

5 My friend _____ me a book for my birthday. (give)

6 Emi _____ a new apartment yesterday. (find)

b Complete the sentences with the past form of the verbs in parentheses. Use the Vocabulary Bank in the Student Book to help you.

1 I _____ my pencil. Can I use yours? (break)

2 About 20 people _____ to my birthday party. (come)

3 Tara _____ the answers to all the questions. (know)

4 Marco _____ a delicious dinner last night. (make)

5 Mr. Gomez _____ for our meal. (pay)

6 Paul _____ a movie star on the street. (see)

7 I _____ an interesting book last month. (read)

8 We _____ French during our trip to Paris. (speak)

4 PRONUNCIATION silent consonants

a **iChecker** Listen and repeat the words with silent consonants.

wou**l**d	cou**l**d	**Feb**ruary	**k**new
two	**wh**at	**wh**o	**w**rong

b (Circle) six more words with silent consonants.

father	(listen)	green	thought
send	news	Wednesday	sandwich
white	why	wrote	swam

c **iChecker** Listen and check. Then listen again and repeat the words.

5 LISTENING

a **iChecker** Listen to a news story about a burglar (a person who goes in a house and takes things). What was the burglar's mistake? Circle a, b, or c.

a He wrote his address.

b He went home by taxi.

c He left his wallet in the house.

b **iChecker** Listen again and write T (true) or F (false).

1 The burglar took laptops from an office. ___

2 The burglar didn't have a car. ___

3 The driver drove White to the police station. ___

4 The police found more laptops in White's house. ___

USEFUL WORDS AND PHRASES

Learn these words and phrases.

<u>bur</u>glar   /'bərglər/

mi<u>s</u>take   /mɪ'steɪk/

jail   /dʒeɪl/

OFFERS AND INVITATIONS accepting and declining

Order the lines to make dialogues.

1

___1___ A Would you like to come for dinner tomorrow?
_____ B Yes, 7:30 is good for me. Can I bring something?
_____ A Great. Is 7:30 OK?
_____ A Oh, OK. Would you like to come on Sunday?
_____ B Yes, I'd love to. Thanks!
_____ A Yes. Bring something to drink.
_____ B Sorry, I can't. Tomorrow is my brother's birthday.

2

___1___ A Hi, John! Come in. Would you like something to drink?
_____ B Uh...No, thanks. I don't like soda.
_____ A OK. Would you like juice?
_____ B Thanks. What do you have?
_____ A I have soda. Would you like a soda?
_____ B Yes, please. Juice is good. Thanks!

2 PRONUNCIATION linking: *would you*

iChecker Listen and repeat the sentences.

1 Would‿you like a soda?
2 Would‿you like to come for dinner?
3 Would‿you like something to drink?
4 Would‿you like to go to a movie?
5 Would‿you like to play soccer tomorrow?
6 Would‿you like salad or a sandwich?

3 KINDS OF PARTIES

Complete the invitations. Choose from the words below.

barbecue	birthday	card	chips
drink	housewarming	soda	

Come to Mark's 18th ¹ _birthday_ party!

When: Saturday, May 8th, 7:00 p.m.

Where: Mark's House, 18 West Street

What: Music and dancing! We'll also drink ² _____ and eat pizza and birthday cake.

Don't bring presents, please. Just bring a birthday ³ _____.

18

Dear Lara,

Maria and Tom moved to their new house last week. It's very nice. Would you like to go to their ⁴ _____ party with me? It's on Saturday evening at 8:00. Let me know!

Talk to you soon,

Chris

P.S. Don't worry about presents. Just bring something to ⁵ _____.

Lisa Yu: Hey Jen, do you like burgers and hot dogs? Come to my ⁶ _____ on Sunday afternoon! Oh, and can you bring potato ⁷ _____?

12A Trip of a lifetime

1 GRAMMAR future: *be going to*

a Write affirmative or negative sentences.

1 Paul / visit Paris [+]
   Paul is going to visit Paris .
2 She / go to work today [–]
   _____ .
3 They / go shopping downtown [+]
   _____ .
4 I / get up early tomorrow [+]
   _____ .
5 Liz / use her laptop today [–]
   _____ .
6 Rodrigo / move to a new house this year [+]
   _____ .
7 We / go to the gym tonight [–]
   _____ .
8 I / make dinner tonight [–]
   _____ .

b Order the words to make questions.

1 are / go / going / Where / to / they
   Where are they going to go ?
2 leave / is / going / What time / the train / to
   _____ ?

3 going / she / How / travel / to / is
   _____
4 you / to / city / going / What / visit / are
   _____
5 are / come home / they / to / When / going
   _____
6 do / Ken / What / to / going / is
   _____

c Look at the pictures. Answer the questions in **b**.

1 *They're going to go to Rio*
2 _____
3 _____
4 _____
5 _____
6 _____

d Complete the dialogue.

Matt Bella, would you like to see a movie next weekend?
Bella I'd love to, but I can't. [1] *I'm not going to be* (not be here next weekend.
Matt Where [2] _____ (you / go)?
Bella To Boston. It's my friend's wedding.
Matt Oh. Who [3] _____ (she / marry)?
Bella A guy from her office. I don't know him.
Matt Where [4] _____ (you / stay)?
Bella We [5] _____ (stay) in a hotel.
Matt [6] _____ (you / fly) there?
Bella No, we [7] _____ (not go) by plane.
   We [8] _____ (take) the train.
Matt When [9] _____ (you / leave)?
Bella On Thursday night. I [10] _____ (not go) to work on Friday.
Matt When [11] _____ (you / come back)?
Bella We [12] _____ (come back) Sunday night
Matt Well, what [13] _____ (I / do)?
Bella I don't know. See a movie?

2 PRONUNCIATION sentence stress

a iChecker Listen and repeat. Copy the rhythm.

1 I'm **going** to **go** by **train**.
2 We **aren't going** to **go** to **work**.
3 They're **going** to **visit Paris** next **week**.
4 She **isn't going** to **travel** a**lone**.
5 He's **going** to **buy** a **house** in the **city**.
6 You **aren't going** to **like** this.

b iChecker Listen and repeat. Copy the rhythm.

1 **Where are** you **going** to **go** for va**cation**?
2 Are they **going** to **visit** the mu**seum**?
3 **What time** are you **going** to **leave**?
4 Is she **going** to **be** there to**morrow**?
5 **How long** is he **going** to **stay**?
6 Are we **going** to be **late**?

3 VOCABULARY future time expressions

a Put the time expressions in order.

_____	tonight
_____	next week
_1_	today
_____	next year
_____	tomorrow
_____	next month
_____	tomorrow night

b Complete the sentences with an expression from **a**.

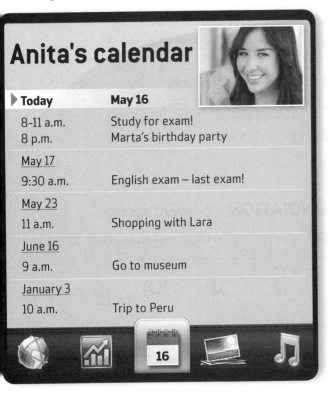

Anita's calendar

▶ Today	May 16
8–11 a.m.	Study for exam!
8 p.m.	Marta's birthday party
May 17	
9:30 a.m.	English exam – last exam!
May 23	
11 a.m.	Shopping with Lara
June 16	
9 a.m.	Go to museum
January 3	
10 a.m.	Trip to Peru

16

1 ___Today___ Anita is going to study for an exam.
2 She's going to go to a party _____ .
3 _____ she's going to take her last exam.
4 She's going to go shopping _____ .
5 _____ she's going to go to a museum.
6 _____ she's going to visit Peru.

4 LISTENING

iChecker Listen to the dialogues and choose a or b.

1 Their trip is going to take about _____ months.
  a six   b seven
2 The woman is going to _____ for vacation.
  a go to the beach   b take a class
3 The woman _____ going to visit her boyfriend in China.
  a is   b isn't
4 The people are going to have a _____ party.
  a housewarming   b birthday

USEFUL WORDS AND PHRASES

Learn these words and phrases.

guy   /gaɪ/
fly   /flaɪ/
exciting   /ɪkˈsaɪtɪŋ/
problem   /ˈprɑbləm/
blog   /blɔg/
penguin   /ˈpɛŋgwən/
climb   /klaɪm/
volcano   /vɑlˈkeɪnoʊ/

12B From start to finish

1 GRAMMAR review of present, past, and future

a Complete the dialogue with the past tense form of the verb.

A What [1] <u>did</u> you <u>do</u> last weekend? (do)

B I [2]_____ (see) a movie and I [3]_____ (visit) my parents.

A Oh. [4]_____ you _____ (have) a good time?

B Yes. We [5]_____ (have) a nice dinner and [6]_____ (watch) TV. How [7]_____ (be) your weekend?

A Good. On Saturday I [8]_____ (not do) anything special. I [9]_____ (get up) late and [10]_____ (read) the newspaper.

B What about Sunday? [11]_____ you _____ (go) to the gym?

A I [12]_____ (not go) to the gym, but my wife and I [13]_____ (walk) in the mountains.

B Really? How far [14]_____ you _____ (walk)?

A I'm not sure. We [15]_____ (leave) at 9:00 and [16]_____ (come) home at 2:00 p.m.

B That's a long walk.

A I know. I'm very tired today.

b Complete the blog with the simple present, present continuous, o
going to form of the verbs.

MY STAYCATION!

Posted by Amanda at 4:30 p.m.

Hi everyone!

I [1] *'m writing* (write) this at my office, so I can't write a long post. We can't write blogs at my job. But my boss [2]_____ (not look) right now!

Anyway, I [3]_____ (want) to tell you about my vacation plans. I [4]_____ (take) a "staycation" next week. [5]_____ you_____ (know) this word? A staycation [6]_____ (be) a vacation, but you stay at home. I usually [7]_____ (go) to the beach for vacation, but not this year. Instead, I [8]_____ (stay) at home for a week and relax. I [9]_____ (get up) late every day. Also, I [10]_____ (read) a lot of books. My friend Susan [11]_____ (take) a staycation next week too. We [12]_____ (make) a big dinner every night.

Right now, I [13]_____ (get) ready for my staycation. I [14]_____ (buy) books online. I [15]_____ (not pack) my suitcase and I [16]_____ (not buy) an expensive plane ticket. It [17]_____ (be) great! Uh-oh, my boss [18]_____ (call) me. Bye!

2 PRONUNCIATION review of sounds

a **iChecker** Listen and repeat the words and sounds.

eɪ train	ɛ egg	u boot	oʊ phone	æ cat	i tree
make play	help send	do you	go snow	have relax	see speak

Circle the word with a different sound.

ei train	1	rain	(man)	same
ɛ egg	2	get	bread	meat
u boot	3	blue	sugar	juice
oʊ phone	4	one	open	hotel
æ cat	5	can	sandwich	take
i tree	6	tea	breakfast	leave

iChecker Listen and check. Then listen again and repeat the words.

VOCABULARY review of verb collocations

Cross out the wrong word or phrase.

1 HAVE   dinner / ~~on vacation~~ / children
2 PLAY   the piano / soccer / a shower
3 TAKE   a mistake / an umbrella / a photo
4 GET   sports / up / a text message
5 GO   home / my girlfriend / to work
6 MAKE   dinner / friends / a photo
7 DO   housework / basketball / homework
8 LEAVE   a bath / the house / your wallet on the bus

b Complete the sentences with the correct form of a verb in **a**.

1 I usually ___*leave*___ home at about 7:30 a.m.
2 We _____ housework on the weekend.
3 Their children _____ the guitar and the drums.
4 I always _____ a coffee at about 10:30.
5 Did you _____ my email? There isn't class today.
6 We usually _____ on vacation in January.
7 Do you usually _____ a shower or a bath?
8 The students sometimes _____ mistakes with their English, but it's OK.

4 LISTENING

a **iChecker** Listen to the answers to an interview with a movie star. What are the questions? Number the questions 1–6.

☐ a What are you wearing right now?
☐ b You're a famous star now. Are you enjoying it?
☐ c What are you going to study?
☐ d What did you do before you were famous?
☐ e Are you going to get married soon?
☐ f Were you a good student?

b **iChecker** Now listen to the interview with questions and answers. Check your answers to **a**.

USEFUL WORDS AND PHRASES

Learn these words and phrases.

special /ˈspeʃl/
I'm not sure. /aɪm nɑt ʃʊr/
boss /bɔs/
instead /ɪnˈstɛd/
online /ɔnˈlaɪn/
get married /gɛt ˈmærɪd/

Listening

1 A 🔊

1 Hello, I'm Tony.
2 You aren't in my class.
3 I'm not a student.
4 Are you in number 5?
5 Sorry, what's your name?
6 You're in class 2.

1 B 🔊

1 A Where are you from?
  B I'm from Mexico.
2 A Where is São Paulo?
  B It's in Brazil.
3 A Where's she from?
  B She's from Peru.
4 A Is he from Korea?
  B No, he isn't.
5 A Is it good?
  B Yes, it's great.
6 A Are you from Vietnam?
  B No, I'm not.
7 A Where's he from?
  B He's from London.
8 A Where's Bilbao?
  B It's in Spain.

2 A 🔊

1 A Are you on vacation?
  B Yes, I am.
  A Great! Where are you from?
  B I'm from Osaka in Japan.
2 A Mmmm. Look. It's pho!
  B Pho? What is it?
  A It's Vietnamese food. And it's
    very good.
3 A Look. Coldplay!
  B They're good. Are they American?
  A No, they aren't.
  B Oh. Where are they from?
  A They're British.

2 B 🔊

1 A What's your address?
  B My email?
  A No, what's your address?
  B Oh, OK. It's 48 Lake Street.
  A 48 Lake Street.
  B Right.
  A Great. Thanks.
2 A What's your number?
  B My home number or my cell phone
    number?
  A Uh, your cell phone number.
  B It's 203-868-5174.
  A Sorry, can you repeat that, please?
  B Yes. It's 203…
  A 203…
  B 868…
  A Uh-huh
  B 5174.
  A 203-868-5174. Thanks.
3 A Excuse me, Mr. Wang, what's your
    first name?
  B My first name?
  A Yes.
  B Uh…it's Shuhao.
  A Oh, how do you spell it?
  B S-H-U-H-A-O.
  A S-H-U-H-A-O.
  B Right.
4 A Welcome to Phone House. How are
    you, sir?
  B Good, thanks. A phone card, please.
  A OK. What's your zip code?
  B My zip code?
  A Yes. What's your zip code, please?
  B Uh, it's 12345.
  A 12345. Really?
  B Yes, really.

3 A 🔊

1 A Look. They're great.
  B Yes, they are. But, uh, what are they?
  A They're gloves.
  B Oh, OK. Yes, they *are* great!

2 A Excuse me, ma'am. What's in your bag?
  B Excuse me? My bag?
  A Yes. Open your bag, please.
  B OK. A laptop, a phone, a wallet,
    and pens.
  A Thank you.
3 A Hi, Robert. Happy birthday!
  B Is it for me? Thanks! What is it?
  A Sit down and open it.
  B A watch! Thanks. It's great!

3 B 🔊

1 A Excuse me. What is this? Is it a toy?
  B No, it isn't. It's a keychain.
  A Oh, OK. It's cute!
2 A Is that for sale?
  B The hat? Yes, that's twenty dollars.
  A Is it from Mexico?
  B Yes, it's a Mexican hat.
3 A Are those sunglasses?
  B Those? Yes, they're sunglasses. They're
    two dollars.
  A Two dollars? Are they good?
  B They aren't *good*, but they're OK.
4 A Are these maps of the city?
  B Yes. They're ten dollars.
  A Ten dollars! That's a lot!
  B They're great maps.

4 A 🔊

1 A That's a cute picture. Is she your
    daughter?
  B No, she isn't. She's my sister's daughter.
  A Oh. How old is she?
  B She's five, and her name is Peggy.
2 A Hi, Tom. Who's the woman in
    the picture?
  B That's Elizabeth. She's in my
    English class.
  A She's very good-looking. Is she
    your girlfriend?
  B Yes, she is.
  A Lucky you!

A Where's my cell phone?
B It's there – on the chair.
A No, that isn't my phone. It's my sister's.
B Oh. Is it in your bag?
A Yes, it is.

A Look. That's Mia's car.
B Is that her husband?
A Yeah. His name's Eric.
B Eric Lee?
A No, that's Mia's last name. His last name is Cho.

A Hey, Jeremy. How's your new car?
B It's great. It's big, black, and fast.
A Is it expensive?
B No, it isn't. It's an old car.

A This is a picture of Jessica's new boyfriend.
B Wow! He's very tall.
A Yes. And he's very good-looking.
B Is he American?
A No, he isn't. He's Italian.

A Is that your son?
B Yes, it is.
A Wow, he's great.
B Thanks. He's small, but he's fast.

A Do you live near here, Julia?
B No, I don't. I live downtown.
A Me, too.

A Do you have children, Steven?
B Yes, I do. I have a son and a daughter.
A Oh, I have a daughter. She's six.
B Really? My daughter is six, too.

A Bob, do you watch MTV?
B No, I don't.
A Do you watch CNN?
B No, I don't. Sorry, I don't like TV. I read books.
A Really? I like TV and books.

A Brian, do you like Mexican food?
B No, I don't.
A Really? But you speak Spanish.
B Yes. I speak Spanish, but I don't eat Mexican food. I like Japanese food.

A Do you like pop music, Liz?
B No, I don't. Do you?
A No. I don't like pop music. I'm old!
B Well, I listen to classical music. Do you?
A No, I don't. I like Brazilian music.

1 A Tony, what do you have for breakfast?
B I usually have toast and coffee. A typical breakfast. How about you?
A Well, my favorite breakfast food is pizza.
B What? Really?
A Yeah. Cold pizza and coffee. It's great for breakfast.

2 A Hi, Lesley. Is that your lunch?
B Yes, it is.
A Wow. A chocolate bar and a soda. That's a small lunch.
B I know. I'm very busy, so I don't eat a big lunch.
A Do you eat a big breakfast?
B Yes, I do.
A Oh, that's good.

3 A Maritza, what do you have for breakfast?
B I have cereal with a lot of fruit.
A Mmm. I like fruit. Do you have coffee or tea?
B I have orange juice.
A Oh. Do you drink coffee or tea?
B No, I don't.

4 A Mmm, pizza! Is that your lunch, Bill?
B Yes, it is. Cheese pizza and a soda.
A Cheese pizza. Do you like pizza with meat?
B Yes, I do.
A Do you eat vegetables?
B Uh, no. I don't like vegetables.

1 A What do you do, Wendy?
B I'm a lawyer.
A That's great. Where do you work?
B I work in an office downtown.
A Do you like your job?
B No, I don't. I work Monday to Friday, and Saturday.

2 A Are you here on vacation, Sonia?
B Yes, I am. I'm from Boston.
A What do you do in Boston?
B I'm a waitress.
A That's great.
B Yes, I like it. I don't work in the mornings!

3 A Where do you work, Brad?
B I work in a school near here.
A Oh. Are you a teacher?
B No, I'm not. I'm an assistant.
A Do you like your job?
B Yes, I do. The people are great.

4 A Where do you work, Mark?
B I work at a hospital downtown.
A Oh. Are you a doctor?
B Well, uh, I'm a nurse.
A Oh, OK. That's good. Do you like it?
B No, I don't. I work very late in the evenings.

A Tony, what time do you get up on weekends?
B I usually get up late – about ten o'clock or ten-thirty. I never get up early. After that, I always take a shower and have a big breakfast.
A Do you have coffee or tea with breakfast?
B Well, actually, I never drink coffee or tea. I usually have orange juice.
A What do you do after breakfast?
B I usually read the newspaper and listen to music.
A Do you do housework?
B Sometimes. But not usually.
A What do you do in the afternoon?
B Nothing special. I sometimes go to the gym.
A What do you do in the evening?
B I always go out with my friends. We usually go to a party and dance!

R = Reporter, J = John

R Good morning. I'm in New York City. It's January 1st, so it's winter, and it's cold, about one degree. People usually stay inside on cold days, but not these people. They swim! This is John Carson and he's in the Polar Bear Club.
J Hello.
R John, how cold is the water today?
J The water is about 8° C.
R That's very cold water. Why do you swim in it?
J It's fun! We like it.
R How many people are in the Polar Bear Club?
J About 30 people. We have men, women, children, old people, a lot of people.
R How often do you swim in the cold water?
J We do this just one time a year, on January 1st.
R And what do you do after?
J I go to a restaurant and have a hot breakfast and a hot coffee.
R I see. Thanks, John.
J You're welcome.

7 B))

A Hello, sir. Welcome to New Orleans. How can I help you?

B Yes, uh, I'm in New Orleans for a day. What can I do here?

A Oh, a lot of things. You can play golf, or you can take a boat trip.

B Hmm. Is it expensive?

A Well, it isn't cheap.

B OK. What else? Can I go to the art museum?

A No, you can't. We have a museum but it isn't open today.

B That's too bad.

A Yes. You can also walk in the park, or you can go to the aquarium.

B The aquarium. That's interesting.

A Yeah. You can see fish, penguins, sea lions, and more.

B How much is a ticket?

A Twenty-one dollars, and you can buy a ticket here.

B Great. Here's twenty-five dollars.

A Thank you. Here's your change.

B Oh, can I buy food at the aquarium?

A No, you can't. But you can buy food here!

B OK. Thanks very much.

8 A))

N = Nick, **T** = Tonya

N Tonya! Hi! We usually don't talk on Saturdays. How are you?

T I'm fine, Nick–

N That's great. I'm good, too. I'm at my brother's house and we're having a family party.

T Oh, that's good–

N Yes, everyone is here. Brothers, sisters, my parents, uncles and aunts. It's my father's mother's birthday.

T I see.

N We're eating grilled meat, fish and vegetables, and my mom is making a salad. Oh, and my aunt is making a birthday cake. The children are playing soccer– they're very cute.

T It sounds like a great time.

N Yes. Now, I'm sorry. Why are you calling? Is everything OK at the office?

T Well, Nick, I'm calling because we have work today.

N Really? But it's Saturday.

T We always go to the office on the first Saturday of the month. Remember?

N Uh-oh. Is that today?

T Yes, it is. Everyone is here, and we're working very hard.

N Oh, no. Tonya, I'm sorry.

T It's OK. But don't forget next month.

N OK. I promise. Oh, we're singing "Happy Birthday" now. Talk to you Monday. Sorry again.

T Bye, Nick.

8 B))

1 A Amy, what do you do?

B I'm an assistant. I work in an office.

A Do you enjoy your job?

B Well, it's OK. But it isn't my dream job.

A So what are you doing today?

B I'm helping my father. He's a vet.

A I see. And how is it?

B Great. I'm helping cute cats and dogs.

2 A What do you do, Marcus?

C Well, I play soccer.

A You're a professional soccer player?

C That's right.

A You already have a great job!

C Well, it's hard work. And I'm getting old.

A I see. You want a new career.

C Yes. After soccer, I want to be a lawyer. So today, I'm working with a lawyer. I'm writing emails and helping her with her papers. It's very interesting.

3 A Steve, what do you do?

D I'm a policeman.

A Do you like your job?

D I like it, but I work on the street. In the rain, in the snow, in the hot weather… That isn't fun.

A And you want to change your job.

D Yes, I want to make computer games.

A Really?

D Yes. I need ideas so I'm playing a computer game now. Look, this game is very good.

9 A))

A Good afternoon. Welcome to Oceanside Hotel. Do you have a reservation?

B Yes, we do. Our last name is Green.

A Welcome, Mr. and Mrs. Green. You're in room 304. That's on the third floor.

B Great. Where are the elevators?

A Uh, actually we're a small hotel. There aren't any elevators.

B That's OK. Can we see the ocean from our room?

A Yes, there's a beautiful view from your room.

B Perfect! Is there a TV in our room?

A No, there isn't, but there are some books and magazines in the room, and you can also use the Internet. Also, there's a TV in the restaurant.

B OK. Oh, and is there a gym?

A There isn't a gym. I'm sorry. But you can swim in the ocean. That's good exercise.

B That's true. Oh, and are there any drinks in the room like juice or soda?

A No, there aren't. But there's a gift shop on the first floor. You can buy drinks there.

B OK. Thanks!

9 B))

1 A Tracy, look at this picture on my phone.

B Wow, that's a famous movie star, right?

A Yeah. He was at the supermarket this afternoon.

B Too bad. I was at the gym this afternoon.

A I guess I'm lucky! He was very nice and friendly.

2 A How was your vacation?

B Terrible! First, we were at the airport for twelve hours!

A Oh, no.

B Our hotel was terrible too, and the beach wasn't clean. The restaurant was bad, too.

A I'm sorry to hear that.

B Yeah. And the weather was cold and windy every day.

3 A Was James at school today?

B No, he wasn't. And he wasn't in school yesterday.

A Oh. Maybe he's sick.

B But he was at the movie theater yesterday evening.

A Hmm. That's strange…

4 A You weren't at home last week. Where were you?

B I was in Paris.

A Paris! Wow. How was it?

B It was great. The food was good, and the views were beautiful.

A How long was your vacation?

B Oh, actually, I wasn't there on vacation. I was there for work.

10 A))

A Sam, how was Nepal?

B It was amazing. I was there for three months, and I changed a lot.

A Where did you live?

B I lived in the city with a host family. They were a mother and father and a son. The son was the same age as me, so that was fun.

What did you do there?

I studied Nepali language. My classes started at eight o'clock every morning and finished at five in the afternoon. I also studied Nepali customs. I learned a lot of Nepali songs.

That's great. How did you travel to school?

I traveled on foot. My host brother traveled by motorcycle, but I didn't want to do that. The traffic was terrifying!

Did you visit the mountains?

Yes, I did. I walked in the mountains for a week. It was very hard work!

How was the food?

Well, the food was OK. It was very basic– rice and vegetables for breakfast, lunch, and dinner. I really missed American pizza! Oh, but I tried a delicious drink called a *lassi*.

What is that?

Uh, it has fruit and yogurt in it, and it's very delicious.

10 B))

S = Steve, **H** = Helena

S Hello? Helena! I'm home!

H Hi, Steve. Did you have a good day?

S No, not really.

H Oh, no. Why not?

S Well, first, my train was late. We had an important meeting this morning, and I wasn't there.

H Oh, I'm sorry.

S How about you? How was your day?

H Very good. I had lunch with my boss at a nice restaurant.

S Really? That's great.

H Yes, I had grilled fish. It was delicious.

S I didn't have lunch. It was a very busy day and I finished work very late.

H I know. It's eight-thirty.

S Sorry. I called to tell you. Did you get my message?

H Yes, I did. Thanks.

S Did you have dinner?

H Yes, I did. I cooked some chicken soup.

S Chicken soup? Mmm. I love chicken soup.

H I know. I cooked it for you. Have some!

S Thanks. My day isn't so bad now.

11 A))

H = Host, **G** = Gia, **R** = Rob

H Hello, this is "Pop Music Today." My guests are Gia and Rob, the singers in a new pop group called Too Cool. Gia and Rob, welcome.

G Thanks.

R Thank you.

H Everyone loves your music. What singers do *you* like?

G I love Lady Gaga. She's fantastic.

R Well…

G But Rob doesn't like her. He thinks she's terrible.

H Really?

R It's true. I prefer rock music. I really like U2. They're fantastic.

H Interesting. Gia, what do you think of U2?

G Um, I don't like them, actually. But I really like their singer, Bono.

R Yeah, Bono's great.

H So Rob loves rock music but Gia hates it.

G Oh, no. That isn't right. I love rock music.

R Yeah, we both love it.

H What about hip hop music?

G It's fantastic!

R I don't like it.

G What? Really? But you really like The Black Eyed Peas.

R That's pop music. It isn't hip hop.

G Well, I love hip hop and I really like The Black Eyed Peas.

H Great. Gia and Rob, thank you!

R You're welcome.

G Any time.

H Next, let's talk to…

11 B))

H = Host, **L** = Luis

H Good morning. This is the news. A burglar went downtown last night and took laptops, cameras, and a TV from a house. But he also made one big mistake, so today he is sitting in jail. The police say Paul White, age 26, went into a house on Fourth Street at about 11:00 last night. He took two laptops, three expensive cameras, a TV, and a woman's bag. The bag had about three-hundred dollars in it.

No one saw White go into the house or leave the house. But White didn't have a car. He couldn't walk home and carry all of the things he took, so he called a taxi. That was his big mistake. The taxi driver drove White to his house. Then he wrote down the address and called the police. The driver, Luis Rodriguez, told us his story:

L "I knew he was a burglar. People don't usually walk around with laptops and TVs at night. Also, he had three cameras in his bag, and it was a woman's bag!"

H After they took White to jail, policemen found more TVs, cameras, cell phones, laptops, and other things in the burglar's house. Now, to sports. Tonight's basketball game…

12 A))

1 **A** Are you going to do anything exciting next year?

B Yes, I am. My wife and I are going to ride our bikes across Canada.

A Wow! How far is that?

B It's about four thousand miles.

A Really? How long is it going to take?

B I'm not sure. It's going to take about six months, probably.

2 **A** Are you going to go anywhere this summer?

B No, I'm not.

A That's too bad. You aren't going to take a vacation.

B Well, I am going to take a vacation, but I'm not going to travel.

A Oh, I see. What are you going to do?

B I'm going to take an art class in the city.

A Really? I didn't know you like art.

B Well, I do. I love art and I want to be a painter. I'm going to have art class every day from nine to three, and after that we're going to go to the museum and study paintings.

A Wow, that's great.

B Yeah. I usually go to the beach, but that isn't very exciting.

3 **A** Hey, Jessica, how are you?

B OK. Well, I have a problem.

A Really? What is it?

B My boyfriend's going to work in China for two years.

A Two years? That's a long time.

B I know. And China is very far from Chicago. I'm going to miss him a lot.

A Are you going to visit him?

B I don't know. I can't speak Chinese, and plane tickets are expensive.

A Well, China is cool. I was there last year. Go visit him. You're going to have a great time.

B Yeah. You're right. I'm going to go. Maybe next year.

4 A The party is going to start at 7:30 tomorrow night. Is everything ready?

B Yes. I'm going to make the cake tonight.

A Great. And I'm going to buy Joe's present tomorrow morning.

B OK. Are you going to buy the red hat or the blue hat?

A Hat? Joe doesn't want a hat. We're going to buy a camera for him.

B We are?

A Yes. Did you get my email?

B Sorry, I didn't. Uh, is the camera going to be expensive?

A No, it isn't. Don't worry.

B Oh, good.

A Are you going to get a card?

B Yes, I'm going to get the card.

A Thanks. I'm going to get soda and potato chips and things.

B Great. See you tomorrow!

12B))

I = Interviewer, **C** = Carrie

1 I Carrie Gold. You're a very famous star now. Are you enjoying it?

C Yes, I'm enjoying it a lot. It's great. I'm wearing these beautiful clothes, and people are taking my picture. It's great. I'm having a great time.

2 I What did you do before you were famous?

C Oh, a lot of things. I was an assistant in an office. I was an English teacher. Oh, and I was a waitress. I worked in a cafe and made cappuccinos. I had a good time there.

3 I Your parents are English teachers. Were you a good student?

C No, I wasn't. I liked my classes and my teachers, but I didn't study hard. I feel bad about it now. Actually, after my next movie I'm going to take college classes.

4 I Really? What are you going to study?

C I'm going to study English and art. I really like art, but I'm not very good at it. I'm also going to take a Spanish class. Hola! Cómo estás?

5 I You have a new boyfriend. Are you going to get married soon?

C No, I'm not. I'm going to get married and have children one day, but I'm not going to get married this year–or next year.

6 I One more question. Your fans want to know this. What are you wearing right now?

C I'm wearing a beautiful red dress by Oscar Saatchi. Oh, and I'm wearing some Italian shoes by Enzo Pisa.

OXFORD
UNIVERSITY PRESS

198 Madison Avenue
New York, NY 10016 USA

Great Clarendon Street, Oxford, OX2 6DP, United Kingdom

Oxford University Press is a department of the University of Oxford.
It furthers the University's objective of excellence in research, scholarship,
and education by publishing worldwide. Oxford is a registered trade
mark of Oxford University Press in the UK and in certain other countries

© Oxford University Press 2013

The moral rights of the author have been asserted

First published in 2013

2017 2016 2015 2014

10 9 8 7 6 5 4 3

No unauthorized photocopying

All rights reserved. No part of this publication may be reproduced, stored in a
retrieval system, or transmitted, in any form or by any means, without the prior
permission in writing of Oxford University Press, or as expressly permitted by
law, by licence or under terms agreed with the appropriate reprographics rights
organization. Enquiries concerning reproduction outside the scope of the above
should be sent to the ELT Rights Department, Oxford University Press, at the
address above

You must not circulate this work in any other form and you must impose
this same condition on any acquirer

Links to third party websites are provided by Oxford in good faith and for
information only. Oxford disclaims any responsibility for the materials contained
in any third party website referenced in this work

General Manager: Laura Pearson
Executive Publishing Manager: Erik Gundersen
Senior Managing Editor: Louisa van Houten
Associate Editor: Hana Yoo
Design Director: Susan Sanguily
Executive Design Manager: Maj-Britt Hagsted
Associate Design Manager: Michael Steinhofer
Image Manager: Trisha Masterson
Image Editor: Liaht Pashayan
Electronic Production Manager: Julie Armstrong
Production Coordinator: Brad Tucker

ISBN: 978 0 19 477638 7 WORKBOOK (PACK)
ISBN: 978 0 19 477602 8 WORKBOOK (PACK COMPONENT)
ISBN: 978 0 19 477668 4 ICHECKER (PACK COMPONENT)

Printed in China

This book is printed on paper from certified and well-managed sources

ACKNOWLEDGEMENTS

*The authors and publisher are grateful to those who have given permission to reproduce the
following extracts and adaptations of copyright material:*

Illustrations by: Cover: Chellie Carroll; Mark Duffin pp.24, 25, 26, 38, 40, 41, 44;
Clive Goodyear p.22, 33, 43, 51, 52; Sophie Joyce pp.8, 17, 48, 54; Jerome Mireault
pp.10, 26, 37, 39; Roger Penwill pp.4, 15, 16, 20, 21, 31, 45, 46; William Waitzman
pp.14, 18, 19, 30, 47.

*We would also like to thank the following for permission to reproduce the following
photographs:*

Cover: Gemenacom/shutterstock.com, Andrey_Popov/shutterstock.com,
Wavebreakmedia/shutterstock.com, Image Source/Getty Images, Lane Oatey/
Blue Jean Images/Getty Images, BJI/Blue Jean Images/Getty Images, Image Source/
Corbis, Yuri Arcurs/Tetra Images/Corbis, Wavebreak Media Ltd./Corbis; pg.6
(Mexico) Robert John/Alamy, (Korea) Tim Hill/Alamy, (Japan) Keith Levit/Design
Pics/Corbis, (USA) Les and Dave Jacobs/cultura/Corbis, (kimono) Ocean/Corbis,
(Canada) Adam Stoltman/Corbis, (vase) Fotosearch Value/Getty Images, (Flamenco
Sawayasu Tsuji/istockphoto.com, (Brazil) Robert Harding Images/Masterfile,
(China, Spain) OUP/Photodisc, (England) OUP/Jan Tadeusz, (sombrereo) Chiyacat/
shutterstock.com, (Saudi Arabia) Kaehler, Wolfgang/SuperStock; pg. 8 Corbis Flirt/
Alamy; pg. 9 (England flag) visual7/istockphoto.com, (All other flags) OUP/Graphi-
Ogre; pg. 11 (hand) Stuart Paton/Getty Images, (woman), Image Source/Getty
Images, (man) Pablo Calvog/shutterstock.com; pg. 12 Jean Glueck/Getty Images;
pg. 13 (1) OUP/Mark Mason, (2) DEA/G CIGOLINI/AGE fotostock, (3) Photononstop/
SuperStock, (4) Patrycja Zboch/shutterstock.com, (5) Dinodia Photos/Alamy, (6)
Spiderstock/istockphoto.com, (7) Seregam/shutterstock.com, (1 down) Ingvar
Bjork /shutterstock, (2 down) Igor Grochev/shutterstock.com, (3 across, 4 down)
OUP/Photodisc, (4 across) OUP/David Brimm, (5 across) Wiskerke/Alamy, (6 down)
Jason Lugo/istockphoto.com, (7 down) OUP, (8 across) OUP/Ingram, (8 right) Karkas
shutterstock.com, (8 left) Stocksnapper/shutterstock.com, (9 across) Antagain/
istockphoto.com; pg. 15 (1) Jami Garrison/istockphoto.com, (2) OUP/Digital
Vision, (3) malerapaso/istockphoto.com, (4) r_alva/istockphoto.com, (5 across)
Stocksnapper/shutterstock.com, (5 down) Thomas Vogel/istockphoto.com, (6)
Ocean/Corbis; pg. 17 Ocean/Corbis; pg. 22 Lew Robertson/Getty Images; pg. 23
Blend Images/Alamy; pg. 24 (1) OUP/Przemyslaw, (2) OUP/igor kisselev, (3 down)
OUP/Photodisc, (3 across) Hakan Dere/istockphoto.com, (4) dabjola/shutterstock.
com, (5) OUP/Photodisc, (6) DustyPixel/istockphoto.com, (7) AntonioFoto/
shutterstock.com, (8) Francesco83/shutterstock.com, (9) Yvan Dubé/istockphoto.
com, (woman top) bikeriderlondon/shutterstock.com, (man middle) Kiselev
Andrey Valerevich/shutterstock.com, (woman bottom) Will Hughes/shutterstock.
com, (man right) Aaron Amat/shutterstock.com; pg. 27 (man top) db2stock/Getty
Images, (man bottom) Winslow Productions/Getty Images, (woman) takayuki/
shutterstock.com, (Mexico) Marka/SuperStock; pg. 28 (1) OUP/Corbis, (2) MBI/
Alamy, (3) OUP/Digital Vision, (4) Glowimages/Masterfile, (5) OUP/Photodisc, (6)
OUP/Image Source, (7) OUP/JinYoung Lee, (8) Hemis.fr/SuperStock, (9) OUP/Digital
Vision, (writer) Daly and Newton/Getty Images; pg. 29 Image Source/Alamy; pg.
30 (man) John Lund/Marc Romanelli/Getty Images, (woman) Dougal Waters/Getty
Images; pg. 32 (beach) Gaia Vittoria Marturano/Alamy, (reporter) PhotoStock-
Israel/Alamy, (man) Three Images/Getty Images; pg. 33 (1,4) pearleye/istockphoto.
com, (2) Tish1/shutterstock.com, (3) Cheryl Casey/shutterstock.com, (5) Image
Farm Inc./Alamy, (6) astudio/shutterstock; pg. 34 (information) picturesbyrob/
Alamy, (a) OUP/Photodisc, (b) NASA/SCIENCE PHOTO LIBRARY, (c, d) NASA/Roger
Ressmeyer/CORBIS; pg. 35 (top left) Jim Goldstein/Alamy, (top right) Tetra Images/
Alamy, (bottom left) NetPhotos/Alamy, (bottom right) OUP/Photodisc; pg. 36 (1)
Greg Hinsdale/Corbis, (2) Matt Hage/Alaska Stock/SuperStock, (3) Jerry Driendl/
Getty Images, (4) Belinda Images/SuperStock, (5) INSADCO Photography/Alamy,
(6) Datacraft - Sozaijiten/Alamy, (7) Bill Sykes/cultura/Corbis, (8) Jeff Greenberg/
Alamy; pg. 38 (museum) Tomas Abad/AGE fotostock, (computer) Blend Images/Hill
Street Studios/Getty Images, (study group) Damir Cudic/Getty Images; pg. 41 Hybrid
Images/cultura/Corbis; pg. 43 Francis G. Mayer/CORBIS; pg. 46 Yevgen Timashov/
beyond/Corbis; pg. 49 (left) Juice Images /Getty Images, (1) Kevin Mazur/WireImage.
(2) Will Hart/NBC/NBCU Photo Bank via Getty Images, (3) Daniel Freytag/Demotix/
Corbis, (4) Mike Coppola/Getty Images, (5) FilmMagic/Getty Images, (6) Stefan M.
Prager/Redferns/Getty Images, (7) George Pimentel/WireImage/Getty Images; pg.
50 (interview) Hill Street Studios/Blend Images/Corbis, (Coldplay) Carlos Alvarez/
Redferns via Getty Images; pg. 53 (2 men) BE&W agencja fotograficzna Sp. z o.o /
Alamy, (woman) Take A Pix Media/Getty Images, (2 girls) michaeljung/shutterstock.
com; pg. 55 (bike) Philip and Karen Smith/Getty Images, (woman) AntonioDiaz/
shutterstock.com; pg. 56 (couple) D. Hurst/Alamy, (woman) Fuse/Getty Images;
pg. 57 Masterfile.